Encountering Ellis Island

How Things Worked

Robin Einhorn and Richard R. John, Series Editors

ALSO IN THE SERIES:

Sean Patrick Adams, *Home Fires: How Americans Kept Warm in the Nineteenth Century*

Encountering Ellis Island

How European Immigrants Entered America

RONALD H. BAYOR

Johns Hopkins University Press | *Baltimore*

Printed in the United States of America on acid-free paper
9 8 7 6 5 4 3 2 1

Johns Hopkins University Press
2715 North Charles Street
Baltimore, Maryland 21218-4363
www.press.jhu.edu

Library of Congress Cataloging-in-Publication Data

Bayor, Ronald H., 1944–
Encountering Ellis Island : how European immigrants entered America / Ronald H. Bayor.
pages cm — (How things worked)
Includes index.
ISBN 978-1-4214-1367-9 (hardback) — ISBN 1-4214-1367-1 (hardback) — ISBN 978-1-4214-1368-6 (paperback) — ISBN 1-4214-1368-X (paperback) — ISBN 978-1-4214-1369-3 (electronic) — ISBN 1-4214-1369-8 (electronic)
1. Ellis Island Immigration Station (N.Y. and N.J.)—History. 2. United States—Emigration and immigration—History. 3. Immigrants—United States—History. I. Title.
JV6484.B39 2014
304.8'7304—dc23
2013036937

A catalog record for this book is available from the British Library.

Special discounts are available for bulk purchases of this book. For more information, please contact Special Sales at 410-516-6936 or specialsales@press.jhu.edu.

Johns Hopkins University Press uses environmentally friendly book materials, including recycled text paper that is composed of at least 30 percent post-consumer waste, whenever possible.

For my grandparents, who arrived in America through Ellis Island
Charles Shapiro and Elke Hamerman
Samuel Banischewitz and Kate Altman

CONTENTS

PREFACE

Millions of immigrants came to the United States in the peak immigration years of 1892–1924, and Ellis Island is where the great majority landed. What happened to them along the journey to Ellis Island, and how did the processing of so many people work? In 1907, over a million immigrants disembarked and entered Ellis Island. On one day in April of that year, almost 12,000 had to be processed. As part of the "How Things Worked" series, this book provides in-depth accounts, by using immigrants' and Ellis Island workers' voices, to offer their view of how the immigration system operated. The immigrants, doctors, inspectors, aid workers, and interpreters, among others, are the focus of this volume—how did the immigrants get to America, react to the Ellis Island inspection, and deal with delays, hospitalization, detention, deportation, food, and sleeping quarters, and how did Ellis Island staff and others involved in the process regard their work and the millions who passed through their inspection lines over the years?

Ellis Island opened in 1892 with a goal of placing immigration under the control of the federal government and systematizing the entry process. This island became the model for all other inspection stations, including Angel Island, the main entry point for Asian immigrants, which is also discussed in this volume. Readers will be able to walk through the whole immigration procedure, picture themselves as one of the immigrants or staff, and get a sense of how it felt to be there. Immigrant emotions included anxiety, depression, excitement, happiness, and boredom, even for those receiving quick entry, and especially for those whose admission faced obstacles.

Immigration history does not only comprise laws and political disputes, nativistic or welcoming attitudes; it is the story of people leaving everything behind, facing a new language and culture, perhaps being sent back to the old country without family or funds, or starting a new American life. I want readers to understand how Ellis Island worked and also how people felt about their experience. Ellis Island had many liabilities and many assets as a processing station. Numerous immigrants often had to deal with corruption, struggled with medical issues, and sometimes faced a hostile staff, but families also reunited in great joy and found profound relief in finally ending their journey. This book describes how the whole system worked and how immigrants and others lived through the process.

I am grateful to various people who helped in the researching and publication of this book. Robert J. Brugger, senior editor at Johns Hopkins University Press, suggested this book to me as part of the new series "How Things Worked" and has been very helpful in making this a better study, even as I grumbled about doing more drafts. My thanks go as well to the series consulting editors Robin Einhorn and Richard R. John and to the anonymous readers who evaluated the manuscript and provided good suggestions.

My trips to Ellis Island brought me into contact with Dr. George Tselos, Ellis Island supervisory archivist and head of Reference Services at the Statue of Liberty National Monument and Ellis Island Immigration Museum, who offered friendly conversation and important help in securing access to the oral history and other collections that provided a gold mine of information. Barry Moreno, librarian and historian at the Ellis Island Immigration Museum, answered questions and aided me greatly through his books on Ellis Island. The Interlibrary Loan staff at Georgia Tech made available the many books and articles needed for my research and did this with much-appreciated speed.

My wife, Leslie N. Bayor, carefully read the manuscript, although she was busy with other tasks, and made many good suggestions on the narrative's flow and construction. I thank her, with love.

The dedication of the book to my maternal and paternal grandparents reflects my appreciation to them for making the difficult decision to leave for America, thereby allowing the whole family a better life.

Encountering Ellis Island

Prologue

As one immigrant waiting to be examined said, "I couldn't enjoy nothing. I was afraid they were going to send me back. And I was dreaming that if they try to send me back, I'm going to fall into the river and die. I couldn't go back." Fear became an overriding emotion on Ellis Island as immigrants faced a new experience.

One could tell immediately upon entering the majestic main building that Ellis Island represented an unusual place. Immigrants did not know what to expect. Nothing could have prepared them for what they saw and felt. An immense crowd formed, with most new arrivals carrying some precious item, such as baggage, feather beds, and baskets, weighing them down as they entered the structure, forcing them to struggle as they walked up the stairs to the Great Hall. Impressive and frightening, the hall rose up two stories, interrupted only by a balcony, with mazes of iron rails on the floor level, large windows, cages off to the sides with people penned up like animals, and electric lights outlining the balcony. Few, if any, had experienced such a place: bright like the outdoors, but still with a somber look.

The newcomers could not help but feel strange. Various languages blended into a confusing roar, and the colorful clothing so many immigrants wore gave the appearance of a gigantic costume party. Pushing and surging crowds, along with the sounds of babies crying, mothers wailing in search of missing children, and staff barking orders to go this way or that, little of which produced any understanding, all prevailed. The place bustled with excitement and anticipation, confusion reigned, and it seemed like a madhouse. "We were driven in herds from one place to another," said one new arrival. Looking down from the balcony surrounding the iron maze, one could describe a sea of people packed together. The combination of food, sweat, vermin, and the crowds of bodies gave the place, as one immigrant observed, "a foul odor."

The questions many had, no one could answer. What was expected of us? Was this America? How long would it take us to get out of here? Why did we ever leave home? Most immigrants appeared to be in a perplexed state, and the doctors and other staff had the easy ability, so it seemed, to immediately exclude them. They could tear a child from a mother's arms and take him or her to an unknown location. One Polish woman "suddenly became aware that she has one less child clinging to her skirts" and did not know what to do. And then one could see the seemingly never-ending lines with immigrants moving along, inching up to the doctors and inspector stations. Efforts to hide injuries, rashes, sick babies, or odd behavior would often fail. Should a bribe be offered, as was the custom in the Old World? What happened to those taken off the line and put into a cage, with a chalk mark on their clothes? It was mayhem, or so it seemed. For many immigrants, time stood still. As one said, "The day I spent on Ellis Island was an eternity."

Much of what the immigrants saw that first day allowed them to understand why others called Ellis Island "the Island of Hope, the Island of Tears." Children were hospitalized for unknown reasons, maybe never to be seen again. Immigrants proved easy prey for crooks, con men, fake inspectors, cheating money changers, and people selling phony citizenship papers. Yet joyful and ecstatic scenes prevailed, with families reuniting after not seeing each other for years, embracing, crying, holding tight. Relatives searched for one another, having forgotten what each looked like after so many years, asking, "Are you my uncle? Are you my brother?" Sobbing with fear at the beginning of the day could turn to laughing with happiness at the end.

The immigration machinery moved along regardless of fear or hope, relentlessly spitting out those deemed unacceptable and pushing along those allowed entry. Ellis Island appeared as a giant mass production factory pouring immigrants into America, a conveyer belt moving masses from boat to barge to inspection. For the immigrants it might be chaos, but for the immigration officials—often handling 5,000 new arrivals a day, and while sometimes appearing to be overwhelmed amid thoughts of being swamped by this ocean of humanity—the system worked well. One interpreter said, "I thought it was a stream that would never end." But a well-trained bureaucracy existed; Congress set the requirements for exclusion, and the immigration staff developed a procedure, with some changes over the years to improve efficiency. Each doctor and each immigration official had their place and purpose. Contagious disease specialists, mental health physicians, interpreters trained in a number of languages, inspectors knowledgeable of questions to be asked, and special inquiry boards hearing appeals were all stationed in that one main building. But how could they process so many immigrants so fast? Doctors became experts at the glance, looking at each immigrant as they walked by on the line in order to determine their physical condition. If the immigrant had a limp, or a curved back, or a missing finger, it had to be determined whether this person could engage in paid work or would become a charity case. Doctors worked diligently all day. Immigrants feared the doctors, especially the one who seemed to be poking out someone's eye. And the doctors dressed in military-type uniforms, as Public Health Service officers, which increased the immigrant's concerns given experiences in the Old World with the military. Some doctors found their work at Ellis Island disturbing. One commented, "I approached my task with considerable misgiving, feeling that I had become part of the crushing mechanism."

Immigrants also arrived at receiving stations in cities such as Boston, Philadelphia, and San Francisco, but Ellis Island in New York Harbor, which started receiving immigrants in 1892, remained the main entry port. Other immigration stations copied Ellis Island's practices. Given the island's numbers and primacy in immigration, this book will concentrate on how that station worked, with some comparison to Angel Island, the main entry point for Asian immigrants.

The following chapters cover a wide range of experiences and emotions of those who lived Ellis and Angel Islands: the journey, often dangerous but always exciting, to the train and to the port; the shipboard adventure, which seemed to last forever, leaving the travelers exhausted and sometimes ill; the arduous examination and questioning. Those detained, hospitalized, deported, losing appeals, or being cheated would never forget the whole encounter. And then, entering America, how did the immigrants feel: hope or disappointment, a sense of having made a mistake or a decision never to look back? One newcomer said that "I could not get over the dirty tenements" and "wondered if America was so wonderful after all that I had heard about it." Another immigrant, exhilarated as he left Ellis Island and headed to New York, remembered that "I laughed, perhaps a bit hysterically . . . I was in New York—in America."

The immigration story embodies one of volatility, hardship, depression, happiness, and confusion. Immigrants came to a place not knowing the traditions, language, living style, or even how to dress. And many came. The worldwide migration extended to many countries, with immigrants also going to Australia, Argentina, Brazil, and Canada. However, the majority of immigrants came to the United States, arriving via Ellis Island; this is the story of how the system for entering America worked. Immigrant and staff voices form the core of this book. What was it like to be there as an immigration commissioner, immigrant, detainee, reject, doctor, inspector, interpreter, or volunteer aid worker? Who tried to cheat the immigrants, and did corruption exist on a large scale? Only those who lived the experience can answer these and other questions.

Ellis Island and immigration represented one of the major controversies of the time, much as immigration, documented or undocumented, does today. America in the early twentieth century needed immigrants but did not want all immigrants. How to bring in the people required for America's factories and farms in a systematic way that would not diminish this country became the main question.

Why should immigration history and the Ellis Island process be studied today? The orderly entry of immigrants resonates as a significant political and social issue in contemporary America. Who should enter and who should not are still major concerns. How our forebears solved this problem is at the heart of this study and indicates that the United States, as a nation of immigrants, has always struggled with the many questions massive immigration raises. Since the 1970s and continuing into the twenty-first century, the United States is once again in the midst of large-scale immigration. These immigrants come from different world areas than those who arrived at Ellis Island in the late nineteenth and early twentieth centuries, but the desire to screen, inspect, and choose is still evident. The lessons learned in an earlier time about disease control, regulation, background checks, job skills, political activity, and family ties are still pertinent to the processing of present-day immigrants, with different experiences in relation to arriving by plane rather than ship and with examinations done overseas rather than in New York Harbor. Americans still look askance at people from certain countries or regions and still worry about who can assimilate. History is not repeating itself, but what occurred earlier can be a guide to understanding immigration issues and American responses today.

1 How (and Why) Immigrants Traveled to America

IMMIGRANTS POURED into the country during the main Ellis Island years, and that, as large immigration numbers do today, worried many Americans. Why were so many arriving? How could they be processed? Should laws be passed to hold back the tide? Did it matter where they came from and what skills they had? How would the future United States population look? Early twentieth-century Americans searched for answers to questions still asked in present times. The years 1892–1924 represent the peak of immigrant arrivals. Up to that time, immigrants had flowed consistently into America, but not at the levels seen in that 32-year period. More than 14 million immigrants came through the Ellis Island inspection station during that time (71.4% of all immigrants entering the United States), and about 250,000 met rejection and deportation. At Angel Island, the immigrant inspection station in San Francisco Bay, about 340,000 immigrants arrived from 1910, when the station opened, to 1940. Deportation numbers are unknown, but Angel Island had significantly higher detention percentages than Ellis Island. How did all these immigrants get to America, and why did they come?

What was happening in the United States and overseas which led not only to an immigration surge but also to a shift in migrant backgrounds? America during these years went through a depression, a major war, and a period of industrial boom. Industrial monopolization, labor strife, class conflict, urban growth, and transportation development characterized the United States. In Europe, emigration was driven by economic decline, an Italian cholera epidemic, religious persecution, and industrialization, which made artisan trades less profitable and reached into all parts of the continent; for Asians, a war in China could be added to these factors. Immigrants who decided to move were not the dregs of Europe or Asia, but rather people who had saved to pay for the trip with the hope of eventually bringing their families over. Or, they intended to go back to the old country with money in their pockets and the hope of buying land. They were pushed as much as they were pulled. Generally the desire for a new beginning and more opportunity led this large immigrant cohort to leave their ancestral homes. Many returned, some as sojourners going back and forth, some returning home permanently. In the 1908–1923 period, almost 10 million immigrants entered the United States, and more than three million returned home. Italians had the highest number of returnees, and Jews the least, because it would mean going back to religious oppression and economic decline for the latter.

Most came poor as peasants, unskilled or semiskilled factory workers, or artisans to an America in need of workers in industries such as steel, meatpacking, clothing, and mining. Although America had periodic economic declines, as in the early 1890s depression, jobs could be found and money made in many cities and rural regions. Wages compared more than favorably to the old country; America's cities with inadequate housing, poverty, and ethnic conflict still promised an improvement, or the hope of one, over ancestral areas.

The long and difficult journey from village to train to ship to barge to Ellis or Angel Island began with hope, fear, anticipation, and at times misery at leaving parents, relatives, friends, and familiar places behind. A fantastic journey awaited those who left, with the unexpected at every turn.

Sometimes the immigrants witnessed the village turning out to say goodbye as they boarded a train for the port city or set out by foot. John Lukasavicius left Lithuania in 1923.

> A day or two before I was to leave for America, we had a big party at my house . . . All the village came to the party and everybody donated as much money as they could spare for my journey . . . Everybody was glad that I was able to go, and . . . I made several promises of presents to my friends after

> I was working in America. My mother cried a little when I was leaving and asked me to be sure and write her all about my father, who had been gone 16 years.

Other times, the immigrants had to leave secretly, trying to avoid a family that did not want them to leave or government officials who disallowed immigration. Either way, they began an arduous period of travel. Not everyone in the town would be positive about leaving for America. Mary Strokonos left Lithuania in 1915 while in her twenties. She related that "my people do not like me to go when I tell them, so I play like fox and no say anything more about plans. Every time I go to market I keep little money for trip. Three, four years go, then one market day I don't go back home." Villagers warned Charles Bartunek, a Czech arriving in America in 1914 after his brother had sent him letters praising his new life in America, not to go. They claimed that the brother was forced to write such letters. "He is really under regulation. He is a slave over there. They'll get you over there and you'll all be slaves." Nonetheless, he left for what he hoped was a better life. Leaving with the probability of never seeing one's family again was difficult and stressful. As Enrico Fino, remembering his departure from his small town in Italy at age 22, said, "My heart aches every time I think about that afternoon when I left my parents and friends to go to the railroad station. My mother kissed me goodbye and then stood by the doorway as stiff as a statue sobbing . . . as I left the house." Julia Goniprow departed Lithuania in 1899. "The day I left home," she said, "my mother came with me to the railroad station. When we said good-bye, she said it was like seeing me go into my casket. I never saw her again." Victor Tartarini left Italy in 1920 to reunite with his father, who had gone to America a few years before. He said that a wedding photo sent by an uncle from the United States illustrated to his Italian family the promise of riches in America. "He had a tuxedo on and my aunt had a beautiful gown. When we saw the tuxedo and her with all the beautiful white veil, it was a big deal. We thought they were so darn rich . . . So everybody thought everybody was rich in America." Other stories described America as a land of riches. Sadie Carilli left her village in southern Italy with her family in 1904, when she was 9 years old. Her father had gone to America a year earlier. She said that those townspeople who were in the United States already wrote "what they had here [in America], and how good it was and . . . they were making a good living . . . and that's the only thing they used to write." A Lithuanian immigrant had no sadness in leaving the Old World and looked forward to America: "As the boat pulled away, I stood looking at the city. Strangely enough, I felt no pangs of homesickness or loneliness. I felt as if I was sailing toward the pot of gold at the end of the rainbow. America loomed before me. Great big America, where fortunes were made overnight and opportunities beckoned at every corner." Leonard Covello, later an esteemed educator and community leader, said his townspeople in Avigliano, Italy, thought it a "big event" when someone came back from America. "Usually the Americano had a huge gold chain spread across his vest, at the end of which reposed some masterpiece of the watchmaker's art—tremendous in size." But as he said later, "Everything emanating from America reached [Italy] as a distortion . . . News was colored, success magnified, comforts and advantages exaggerated beyond all proportions."[1]

Benjamin Erdberg, a Jewish individual who left Russia in 1905, gave his straightforward reason for emigrating: "Those days everybody's dream in the old country was to go to America. We heard people were free and we heard about better living . . . I was the first to leave from my family. My father didn't want me to go." Benjamin was 17 when he left and already had a skill as a tailor.[2] For many Russian Jews, the reason for leaving would be an obvious one. Although the voyage was difficult for all immigrants, the decision to leave was not always a hard one, especially for Jews from this region. John B. Weber, the first immigration commissioner at Ellis Island, led a five-member investigative committee in 1891 to study the conditions in Europe which led to emigration to the United States. During his trip to Russia, along with committee member Dr. Walter Kempster, he began to understand why such a large Jewish migration out of that country occurred and quoted an emigrant saying, "I am going to America because in that direction lies hope. Here I have only fears to confront me. The hope may prove delusive, but here the fears are certainty. My great ambition is to breathe at least once the free air with which God has blessed the American people." Weber, astonished at the conditions of the Russian Jews and the government's harsh treatment of these people, described their "emaciated forms, the wan faces, the deep sunken cheeks, the pitiful expression of those great staring eyes reminding one of a hunted animal."[3] The Russian government wished to eliminate its Jewish population in one way or another, and Jews ran from the religious/ethnic bigotry and enforced poverty. While American restrictionists (individuals supporting less immigration) worried about the large numbers of

Russian Jewish paupers who were heading to the United States by the 1890s, Weber's report expressed that there was little to worry about for these people, once immigrated, would be able to overcome the poverty brought on by conditions in Russia. As Weber and his fellow committee member describe the immigrants, "A person who by reason of unexpected misfortune or persecutions is deprived of his accumulations, who has been subjected to pillage and plunder while fleeing from the burdens which have become unbearable, if capable of supporting himself and family . . . with a reasonable certainty after obtaining a foothold, and that foothold is guaranteed by friends or relatives upon landing or strong probable surrounding circumstances, is not, according to our definition a pauper."[4]

Many Americans repeatedly raised concerns about all immigrants and their potential for becoming charity cases. Weber implored the American public to understand why these immigrants were poverty stricken and how they would correct their situation. Other committee members, less optimistic about European migration in general, expressed apprehension over competition with American labor and the entry of unfit individuals.

Likewise, Chinese immigrants, mainly from southeast China, left to seek a better life in America, propelled by the despair at home due to economic problems, by social unrest, and in the 1930s by war with Japan. As with the Europeans, some viewed America in idealistic terms, with the Chinese referring to it as the Gold Mountain. Others simply wanted work in an industrializing United States. Hop Jeong, arriving at Angel Island in 1940 at age 10, said, "I knew nothing about America. All I learned from my grandfather, who'd come back from San Francisco, was that this was the land of opportunity, of gold, and of free education." Another Chinese immigrant remarked in 1933 that "they told me that anyone who came through *Gam Saan* [Gold Mountain] will make money fast and go home a rich man." He continued that "anyone who comes to America is well respected in China. My family pushed me to come. They wanted me to make a better living." Mr. Quan, who made the voyage in 1913 at age 16, commented that everyone who came back from America was rich. "They never told me about confinement on Angel Island. That's why people spent all their money to get here . . . thinking in a year or two they'd make it all back."[5]

Among the millions who arrived in America, many encountered incidents of struggle and hardship as a result of their choice to leave the Old World.

For some Europeans, leaving the country signified the first, often very difficult, step. In Russia, Jews had to get past the border guards by any means available, including bribes, in order to get to Bremen, Germany, or other port cities. Leon Solomon, a young Jewish child leaving Lithuania, noted that he and others had to hide in a barn at the border and keep quiet. As he relates, "At the appropriate moment, when those who were experts in helping emigrants across the border, when they thought it was safe, they called to us and said, 'Now, run!' "[6] And the group ran across the border. In another situation, a Jewish emigrant said that "the crowd was told that in the dead of night they would be permitted to slink across the border provided they paid for the privilege. This they had expected, but what they were not prepared for was the fording of a stream. They were also told to be very cautious, to make no noise, and get over as quickly as possible. Terror lent impetus to swift movement and [I] made a dash for the opposite bank." Frieda M., a Jewish child fleeing from Russia with her mother, said that they had to spend the night at a farm while traveling and "a bandit group entered and tried to abduct an eighteen-year old cousin traveling with them." "And my mother stood in front of her and wouldn't let her go . . . They were going to kill my mother," but soldiers arrived at the last minute and saved them. Traveling was particularly dangerous for young women. Hilda S. and her sister, ages 17 and 21, respectively, along with other townswomen, found trouble when they entered Warsaw. Promising to take them to their relative's house in the city, a carriage driver instead took them unbeknownst to a bordello. As Hilda relates,

> We came in, the door is open, and there's a houseful of people, at three o'clock in the morning! There are mattresses all over the floor . . . So we ask for our relative and they say, "He's asleep. You'll see him in the morning. Why wake him up? Wouldn't you like something to eat and drink?" We looked at each other and we were frightened. My sister and the other girl said, "Something is fishy here. Don't eat anything, don't drink anything, and don't get undressed." We huddled—all of us got into a corner. And whatever they said to us, we said "We want to see that man." We never saw the relative. So my sister and the other girl said, "We're going to try to get away to get help." All of a sudden a young man comes over and takes my hands in his and says, "Oh, you have such beautiful hands." And I grabbed my hands away and said, "Don't touch me!" It got light and my sister and

> the other girls weren't there. Then the bell rings and my sister walks in with the other girl . . . and a reporter from a daily Jewish newspaper in Warsaw and a policeman.[7]

The police arrested the proprietors of the house. "It was in the papers. It was a place where they took the girls and they sent them into white slavery! This is exactly what it was. They were going to send us to South America." White slavers kidnapped, seduced, or otherwise forced girls into prostitution.

Getting to ports in Germany meant going past German border guards as well. In 1907, German border guards refused entry to approximately 12,000 Russians, mostly Jews, at the German border owing to the lack of a steamship ticket or money to make the journey to America. In Italy, a villager traveling by train would first see the ship bound for America in Naples or Palermo. Mario Vina, arriving from Italy in 1909 at age 11, as with many other immigrants from various areas, had never seen a ship or the ocean before.[8] Some left family behind and would send for them later; some, such as Elke Hamerman, who left her home shtetl (small Jewish town) in Austria-Hungary in 1909 at age 16 and traveled to America alone, expected to meet her sisters who had come earlier. Others brought family along but feared that all would not be admitted. Samuel and Kate Banischewitz, moving from Warsaw, had to stop in England to deliver their first child before landing in New York, where they had five more.

Compelled by poverty, pogroms (Russian government-sanctioned attacks against Jews), lack of opportunity, war, compulsory military service, suppression of religious or cultural life, or the hope of a better life, and spurred on at times by overenthusiastic letters from family, friends, or townspeople who had gone before and proclaimed the benefits of American life, the immigrants set out.

How to Decide Who Could Enter the United States

In examining the transition from an America in which immigrants largely entered with few restrictions to an America that became more and more exclusive, this story brings us an understanding of what type of immigrant the United States sought. Concerned with problem immigrants and reflecting a national awareness of increasing immigration, New York along with other port cities and Congress began to take a closer look at the immigration issue. As a result, Congress passed various immigration laws, beginning with the Page Act in 1875, which was directed at suspected criminals and prostitutes. The Page Act's purpose was to restrict the immigration of Chinese and other Asian women, often accused of being prostitutes. Politicians in western states mainly supported the law. The concern with Chinese immigration, illustrated by anti-Chinese violence on the West Coast and city and state laws directed against the Chinese, finally led to the 1882 federal Chinese Exclusion Act, which barred Chinese laborers for 10 years and which Congress reaffirmed until the 1940s. The Chinese Exclusion Act, passed to prevent most Chinese immigrants from entering, became the first major immigration law that was clearly racist. Acts in 1882 also excluded convicts, lunatics, idiots, or persons likely to become a public charge (in need of public or private charity). The law also required a head tax on each immigrant.[9]

Prior to federal legislation, state laws governed immigration matters but did little to regulate immigration except in cases in which ships had to be quarantined as a result of illness on board. Laws existed, although rarely implemented, barring the very poor and lawbreakers. As large numbers of Irish and Germans began to arrive at American ports in the 1830s, the admittance process became more standardized and controlled. At the New York City port, the immigration station called Castle Garden, an old fort, opened for processing in 1855. Since the states, especially New York, had been beset with the medical and economic problems of new arrivals, further legislation was passed. The immigration of southern and eastern Europeans beginning in the 1880s provided the impetus for both new federal legislation and the replacement of Castle Garden with the federally run Ellis Island.

The 1891 Immigration Act put all immigration under federal charge. This legislation required medical inspection upon arrival in the United States, set up the inspection process, reaffirmed and expanded the exclusionary categories, established Boards of Special Inquiry for immigrants who wished to appeal decisions, and created a federal Bureau of Immigration. The act added contract laborers, those with loathsome or dangerous contagious diseases, polygamists, those convicted of a crime or guilty of moral turpitude (such as adultery or cohabitation), and insane individuals to the excludable category. Further laws in 1893, 1903, and 1907 required immigrant inspections at the departure port and careful checking of ship manifests; forbade the immigration of anarchists, or anyone who wished to overthrow the government; added to the medical, public charge, and criminal restrictions; and provided for a fine for shipping companies that allowed immigrants with loathsome or dangerous contagious diseases to sail to the United States. A 1917 law added a controversial literacy test (in any language) to the inspection process, as well as including further excludable types. The act also created an "Asiatic Barred Zone" in order to further exclude Asian immigrants, especially from South Asia. A temporary 1921 law set up nationality quotas, and Congress authorized it again in 1922 and 1923. Finally, the immigration flow into the United States declined significantly with the National Origins Act of 1924, set to go into full effect in 1929. Eugenics, or so-called racial science, made race (nationality) a significant factor in this law's targeting of southern and eastern Europeans and Asians, although other Europeans received lower quotas as well. This law set discriminatory restrictive quotas and temporarily ended a period of massive immigration into the United States, until a new law was passed in 1965.

Why all these restrictive laws, and what did they mean for America and for the immigrants? Although the country needed workers for its factories and farms, Americans did not want every immigrant. They had to be healthy and willing to work. Inspections allowed entry to those who could become able workers and contribute to the economy of an industrializing America.[10] Immigrants physically or mentally disabled and thought incapable of performing useful labor should not enter. Variability existed in the medical exams, and inspectors could allow or deny entry on a whim.

Factors such as how immigrants looked, what sort of disability they had, whether it would interfere with their work, and how the immigrant fit into the industrial labor force took on significant importance. Race, nationality, religion, and ethnicity, however, also became major parts of the criteria and shaped the immigration laws over the years. Would the immigrants or their offspring cause a decline in America's fitness as a people or in some way impair the American "race," meaning Anglo-Saxons? In the case of Chinese and other Asian immigrants, generally considered unable to assimilate, race trumped all else, whether they entered through Ellis Island or Angel Island and whether considered able workers or not. This group had the most severe restrictions and was clearly treated differently than European immigrants. Reasons for exclusion corresponded to the needs, values, and prejudices of the times; they would not necessarily be the criteria used today. Furthermore, the understanding of mental defects and of chronic disease was rudimentary.

Most importantly, the United States did not want immigrants who might become public charges, that is, those who would depend on charity for sustenance or be placed in a public institution as a result of age, physical or mental deficiency, criminal behavior, or other factors. If such conditions occurred after entry, the immigrant could be deported for up to three years following arrival. Often, likely to become a public charge became a way to exclude immigrants who appeared to be acceptable but whom inspectors, based on little other than their own opinion, wanted to exclude. William Williams, commissioner of immigration at Ellis Island in the early years of the twentieth century, commented that immigrants must show some desire to improve themselves and the country. He spoke of a Russian family of eight members who were questioned about their intentions in America. The father said that all they wanted was a small room to live in and had no desire for a fortune or a substantial house. Williams thought that this answer showed a lack of initiative and industry, and he deported them.[11]

Even those generally favorable to immigration, such as Theodore Roosevelt, worried about the loss of the American character if too many foreigners were allowed into the country. The people coming through Ellis Island or Angel Island had to be the "right" immigrants for America. But controversy existed over what that meant, except in the case of the Chinese and other Asians, who were expressly singled out as not desirable. Not unlike contemporary views of immigration, a love-hate relationship existed in regard to immigrants: the country needed them for growth, but only some were wanted.

The eugenic theories also coincided with a growing desire to regulate during the Progressive Era. Turning to government to solve societal problems, Americans during this period sought ways to control industry and immigration, as well as impose numerous regulations on other government functions. They saw a country troubled by political corruption, aggressive and overpowering industrialists, excessive competition, union strife, radicalism, uprisings among farmers, an epidemic of lynching in the South, and a political system that no longer seemed to work well. The desire to create an efficient government free from corruption, a well-working industrial system, and a society that was conflict free and took into consideration the plight of the poor led to numerous Progressive Era laws, including antitrust acts, good government campaigns, city reform movements, workmen's compensation, and women's right to vote. A changing America needed to confront the problems brought on by these changes, but not all laws and reform movements were beneficial. Some, such as Prohibition, pushed the country into more crime. And immigration laws could be patently bigoted. Nonetheless, this impulse could be readily seen at Ellis Island, where the United States implemented a smooth, almost mechanized, operation of immigration examination and put immigration regulatory laws into practice. If not for a significant need for workers, both on farms and in industry, and the Progressive Era's impetus for reform, the immigration quota laws based on nationality passed by Congress in the 1920s probably would have occurred much earlier.

Nativist (anti-immigrant) organizations such as the Immigration Restriction League (established in 1894) and various eugenics groups concerned with breeding pushed Congress for more restrictions. Prescott Hall, one of the founders of the Immigration Restriction League, felt forcefully that immigration of southern and eastern Europeans would be detrimental to the country. He suggested that as science has developed ways to breed plants and animals, so should it be involved in human breeding. Therefore, selecting eugenically fit immigrants became crucial to the survival of the United States. Hall and others like him had little faith in the ability of the environment to improve people. Opinions such as Hall's appeared in the public media as well. *Leslie's Weekly*, a popular magazine, spoke directly to the nativist concerns in 1902: "Those of the poorer class are often grimy and strangely and shabbily dressed, although numbers of the women wear bright and picturesque costumes. These include Italians, Russian Jews, and several other nationalities. They appear generally to be of a low order of knowledge, if not intelligence, as well of physical development. The better class, comprising natives of Great Britain, Germany, and Scandinavia, frequently are as well attired as are average Americans. Better developed physically, and mentally superior to the former class, they are more desirable acquisitions to American citizenship."[12]

Anglo-Saxon elites expressed concern about the threat to their group and way of life. In their own words, they embodied the top of the evolutionary chart and did not want so-called inferior peoples in America. These attitudes affected the examinations at Ellis and Angel Islands and placed a very narrow definition on who could be an American.

Prejudices against the Chinese revealed more hostility. The Workingmen's Party of California, started in 1877 by Denis Kearney, an Irish immigrant, had as their slogan "The Chinese Must Go!" On the other side, the National Liberal Immigration League (1906) worked for easier entry for all immigrants. The country witnessed little support for the largely mild restriction policy of the period before 1875 or a total restriction approach except with regard to the Chinese.

During the years from 1899 to 1937, about 143,000 largely Caribbean blacks (less than 1% of total immigrants) also entered Ellis Island and came into an America where racism toward this group reigned throughout the country. Concerned with Europeans and Asians, American restrictionists did not target black immigration.[13]

Although the Statue of Liberty had Emma Lazarus's poem inscribed on the inside of its pedestal in 1903, welcoming "the wretched refuse" of other lands, these are neither the people whom the United States wanted nor largely the people who came. Those arriving on America's shores were pioneers looking for a better life, either by staying in the United States or by returning to their country after making money in the New World. They yearned for a new start, and that is why the entry process could be so traumatic. Chinese and other Asians felt the same yearning on the West Coast at Angel Island, but there prejudice often overrode a desire for workers. Restriction and exclusion characterized the key policies at San Francisco even prior to the opening of Angel Island. In this case, racial factors overrode most other considerations in the entry process. Wretched conditions and a strong opposition to allowing Chinese immigrants into the United States made Angel Island the real Island of Tears.

Port of Departure

Concerns about immigrants' health had risen quickly owing to epidemics and fear regarding the admittance of those who could become public charges and charity cases. Terence Powderly, the U.S. commissioner-general of immigration, made this point in 1902 when he warned that immigration should not make the United States "the hospital of the nations of the earth."[14] Successive laws, by 1907, made the shipping companies responsible for transporting back, at the companies' expense, not only prospective immigrants deported at entry but also those who had resided for up to three years in the United States. Laws mandated fines and forced the companies to maintain detailed manifest lists and to inspect passengers at the departure port. In response, the main companies placed this burden on their shipping agents, making them accountable for those immigrants they signed up for the voyage if a deportable factor had been discovered. If the immigration inspectors ordered back too many immigrants, the agent could lose the right to represent the shipping line. The medical exam's intensity increased during the peak immigration years, and the number of questions the arrivals had to answer became more intrusive. As a result, the journey emerged as already harrowing before the actual ship travel. Some immigrants were rejected at the port; some never tried to leave owing to fear of being rejected after spending so much of their savings to get that far. Exclusions at departure ports increased. According to one journalist who studied immigration, in 1906 approximately 68,000 potential immigrants faced rejection at the main ports in Germany, England, Italy, and Austria-Hungary; about 6 percent were refused boarding at Naples alone. In 1911, government estimates indicated that those denied entry at American ports were about 10 percent of those excluded at departure ports.[15] Overseas inspection of Asian immigrants started earlier, had the highest rejection rates, and served to inspire these procedures at European departure points. These rejection numbers do not include those who decided not to emigrate owing to the possibility of exclusion.

Mary Antin, who later became a celebrated author, wrote of her arrival in Berlin in 1894 on the way to a port. The immigrants' luggage was "steamed and smoked" to eliminate any threat of disease. Officials then moved immigrants into a small house and then a yard, separated by gender and put into a small room where they had to remove their clothes. "Our clothes taken off, our bodies rubbed with a slippery substance . . . a shower of warm water let down on us without warning; again driven to another little room where we sat, wrapped in woolen blankets" until their clothes were returned. When she went to Hamburg, another stop on the way, "we were once more lined up, cross-questioned, disinfected, labeled, and pigeonholed."[16] It took her six weeks to go from Russia to America, with only 16 days on the ship. Antin's experience was a common one. A Slovak woman setting out in 1920 from Prague to Rotterdam, Holland, recounted her journey:

> We were marched to the barracks near the railway station and there were sent into compartments with walls of canvas and told to undress. Our dresses were put on hangars and sent to the disinfection plant. We walked to another room wrapped in blankets . . . A woman with a bucket and a large brush such as used in whitewashing, brushed our bodies from neck to feet with a strong carbolic disinfectant . . . After this we were sent under a hot shower bath and given soap and a towel to wash our bodies. Then a

> woman with a bucket of crude oil came to apply the oil to our heads . . . We were told we could wash our heads in the morning . . . As long as there were any vermin on our heads, we could not depart.[17]

At Rotterdam, doctors checked the eyes and head. Also, the shipping line had built quarters for immigrants arriving in Rotterdam. The building's interior mimicked the steerage area on a ship so that the travelers would acclimate to such conditions before sailing. Fannie C., a 9-year-old arriving in Dansk with her mother, went through a worse examination. As a result of an epidemic, the officials in that city shaved off the hair of all female travelers. "'It was an experience I shall never forget, because I had a beautiful head of hair as a child—all curls. And when I took a look at myself in the mirror, I became hysterical . . . And by the time we reached the boat, anything that would come along just didn't matter any more, because I was already so terribly upset."[18]

Paulina Caramando, who came to America in 1920 when she was 8 years old, remembers that when arriving in Naples from Sicily she "slept in this big hall of the steamship company" and went through a medical examination there. "My father had a friend with his wife and a little boy that were coming also. We were all together. And it was heartbreaking. They were crying. The steamship company wouldn't let them on the boat. They were turned away."[19] Of course, those turned away at the port could try to leave through other ports or with ships where inspections were not as careful, or they could try to enter the United States through Mexico or Canada, which had less intensive examinations.[20]

Additionally, the departure port was a place where immigrants could be cheated and mistreated. Items could be stolen from the immigrants, luggage lost, and travelers swindled out of needed funds or treasured belongings as a result of excessive lodging or ticket costs. Crooked money exchangers, white slavers (pimps), and thieves waited for the immigrants to arrive. Hotels were overcrowded. Pickpockets were numerous. One trick in Italy was to tell immigrants that they could avoid medical inspection if they paid to have their ticket stamped that an American doctor had already given them an exam. Some were convinced to buy phony U.S. citizenship papers in hopes of an easy entry into America. Many immigrants, as first-time travelers who had never been away from their small village, became prime targets for such scams. In general, the port city experience was upsetting. Furthermore, immigrants from Russia and Italy were suspicious of authority figures, who, as they had learned from their life experiences, could not to be trusted. This attitude affected their encounters with inspectors at Ellis Island.[21]

Chinese immigrants encountered scams as well when they sailed from Hong Kong, Canton, or other southern Chinese ports. Inns in departure ports often cheated the immigrants. Since immigrants received a pre-board screening to see if they would pass the medical examination in America, many rejections occurred. In some cases, the doctors extorted money from the immigrants before allowing them to board. The American vice-consul in Hong Kong, John Birge Sawyer, wrote in 1915 about complaints regarding one doctors' group that claimed cures for immigrant patients, only to have them return again and again for more treatment after being barred from the United States and Canada.[22]

At these departure ports, ship manifests recorded immigrants' names along with such information as gender, age, marital status, occupation, literacy, physical condition, criminal record, charity, polygamy, anarchist background, race/nationality, money on hand, who paid for the passage, where they were traveling from and final destination, and people slated to meet them in America (with address). The provision regarding funds on hand related to the fact that immigrants had to have some money to be accepted into America. The amount varied but could be more for the elderly. This entry condition served to prevent paupers who could become a public charge from entering. Other questions asked also related to eligibility.

Names, as recorded on the ship manifest, were not changed at Ellis Island. These manifest names had to be the same through the entire inspection process. Contrary to myth, if immigrants did change their names or shipping officials did so, it occurred at the boarding of the ship at the departure point or after they arrived in America and wished to anglicize their names.

On Board

Most immigrants bound for America sailed in the steerage area, below decks. Steerage was the least desirable space on the ship: an extremely crowded area with inadequate sanitation, no ventilation, noxious smells, noise from the engine and people, and an increased sensation of the rocking of the ship, plus little to do to occupy time. Immigrants slept in two-layer bunks in crowded areas. Three compartments made up steerage: for men traveling alone, for families, and for women without male companions.

Often, passengers stayed on deck during the day, weather permitting. Sometimes the crew would hose down the steerage floor, and the passengers had to go on deck. Edward Steiner, who traveled often on immigrant ships to report on the travel conditions, had this to say about steerage in 1906: "The steerage never changes, neither in location nor its furnishings. It lies over the stirring screws, sleeps to the staccato of trembling steel railings and hawsers. Narrow, steep and slippery stairways lead to it. Crowds everywhere, ill smelling bunks, uninviting washrooms—this is steerage. The odors of scattered orange peelings, tobacco, garlic and disinfectants meeting but not blending. No lounge or chairs for comfort, and a continual blend of tongues—this is steerage." A 1910 congressional committee's report further clarified the world of steerage: "filth and stench . . . added to inadequate means of ventilation . . . In many instances, persons, after recovering from seasickness continue to lie in their berths in a sort of stupor." Another description from a female investigator noted that the toilets for women "were filthy and difficult of use and were apparently not cleaned at all the first few days." She continued that "everything was dirty, sticky, and disagreeable to the touch. Every impression was disagreeable."[23]

As Peter Mossini, who sailed in 1921, relates, officials gave each immigrant a pillowcase that contained eating utensils, a dish, and a cup. To secure food, the group stood in line and received soup, meat, bread, and coffee two times a day.[24] Sometimes the food was placed on a table. The meat would be either boiled beef, salt pork, sausage, stewed liver, corned beef, mutton, or roast beef. However, some had no interest in food, and the quality of the food depended on the shipping line. Steiner reported that "the food, which is miserable, is dealt out of huge kettles into the dinner pails provided by the steamship company. When it is distributed, the stronger push and crowd, so that the meals are anything but orderly procedures. On the whole, the steerage of the modern ship ought to be condemned as unfit for the transportation of human beings."[25] Many experienced seasickness and arrived at Ellis Island weak and malnourished. Rose Vartone, arriving in 1924 from Italy when she was 23, said that it took nine days to sail to America and "nine days I was sick. Nine days I didn't eat nothing, I was sick every single day."[26] Mary Zuk, arriving in 1912, said, "It was so rough! Oh God, it was so rough! I didn't see a thing. A lot of time you just lay in your bed when you don't feel so good. You don't get up and go because if you do you get dizzy and then you get worse sick . . . Oh the waves! . . . I thought the ship would turn over." Mary Strokonos from Vilna, Lithuania, came in 1915 and said of her journey, "When boat sail I am downstairs in boat. Many, many people down there, very crowded. Everybody was sick. I am so sick I cry and cry, I think I die, then I wish I back on farm."[27]

Of course, many people remained well during the passage. For Jewish immigrants who only ate kosher foods, once they ran out of the food they brought along, they would not eat anything else. Many immigrants faced an even worse fate. The *Titanic* sailed in 1912 with numerous immigrants in third class (steerage). Theresa Gavin Duffy from Ireland tried to secure space on the *Titanic* but was denied since the ship was overcrowded. "We got in the small boat to go out to the big ship. When we got to the door, the captain opened it and said, 'No more. Overcrowded.' We were kind of disappointed, but it was the next day when she went down." Waiting two more days for another ship, she sailed safely to America. Chinese immigrants going to San Francisco had similar steerage stories. One traveler said that "in those days, they treated us Chinese like cattle." Another remarked, "I was not used to the wind and waves and was seasick in bed the entire voyage."[28] Ellis Island statistics in 1907 illustrated the journey's horror for some: "1,506 children have been received at this station afflicted with measles, diphtheria, and scarlet fever, all of which diseases are due, more or less, to overcrowding and insanitary conditions. Of this number 205 died."[29] Ellis Island doctors understood the detrimental aspects of steerage and, if necessary, tried to give the immigrants time to recover before their final medical examinations.

Trying to put a more positive spin on the voyage and encourage immigration, one immigrant guidebook described the voyage as "a kind of hell that cleanses a man of his sins before coming to Columbus' land."[30] Yet not everyone had a terrible journey. The experience depended on the ship, the weather, the crew, and whether one could avoid getting seasick. Bessie Spylios, arriving as a child in 1909 from Greece, related how much fun she had on board. "There were about fifty people from the same village and they came at the same time. It was just like a family, we knew each other . . . It was very nice. No, it [the voyage] didn't bother me at all . . . I ran up and down. We had the bottom of the boat for sleeping, but I never stayed there, just when it was bedtime. They had to chase me downstairs to go to sleep." She continued that "they used to yell at me not to run up and down, but there was no fear . . . I was free as air going up and down the stairs . . . having a heck of a time."[31]

Since the shipping companies and their agents had financial responsibility for those rejected and, later on, hospitalized in America, they tried to make sure that their passengers secured entry. As a result, and owing to pressure from American immigration officials, medical inspections in Italy and elsewhere improved over the years. Medical inspections also took place during the voyage, and hospital facilities were offered as needed. The shipping agents also reviewed any questions the Ellis Island inspectors might ask and provided suitable answers for the immigrants, who made sure to memorize exactly what to say.[32] Many immigrants therefore had some sense of what sort of interrogation to expect, but they still remained fearful that a mistake would lead to rejection.

Broughton Brandenburg, an American journalist, traveled with and wrote about the voyage of Italians to America in 1903. Regarding the concern over questions to be asked at Ellis Island, he writes, "I saw more than one man with a little slip of notes in his hand carefully rehearsing the group in all that they were to say when the time came for examination, and by listening here and there I found that hundreds of useless lies were in preparation. Many, many persons whose entry to the country would no way be hindered by even the strictest of enforcement of the letter of the emigration laws, were trembling in their shoes, and preparing to evade or defeat the purpose of questions which they had heard would be put to them."[33] For the steamship companies in 1907, the hospital cost to treat 1,506 sick children was over $104,000.

Most European immigrants thought that their journey's end came with arrival in New York Harbor and the sighting of the Statue of Liberty, but more reasons for trepidation appeared soon. Immigrants had heard of the statue in Europe, but seeing it often brought out strong emotions. Arnold Weiss, a Jewish immigrant from Poland in 1921, said that "seeing the Statue of Liberty was the greatest thing I've ever seen. It was really something. What a wonderful sight. To know you're in this country."[34] Sarah Asher remembered that the statue "was beautiful with the early morning light. Everybody was crying. The whole boat bent toward her because everybody went out, everybody . . . was in the same spot."[35] Angelina Palmiero, who made the crossing at age 10 in 1923, added, "And somebody yelled, 'the Statue of Liberty, the Statue of Liberty!' We all ran to the railing to see, and everybody was praying and kissing and happy that we were coming up the Hudson." Louis Adamic, arriving from the Slovenian part of the Austro-Hungarian Empire in 1913, and later an important American author and journalist, described the scene as his ship entered New York Harbor: "people of perhaps a dozen nationalities milling around the capstans and steam-hissing winches, pushing toward the rails, straining and stretching to catch a glimpse of the new country, of the city; lifting their children, even their infants, to give them a view of the Statue of Liberty; women weeping for joy, men falling on their knees in thanksgiving, and children screaming, wailing."[36] Sometimes, it was not the statue that caught the immigrants' attention but the lights from New York's buildings. Celia Adler, a 12-year-old arriving in 1914, said, "One little boy . . . was the first to see the lights of America, and he came running down [to steerage] screaming, 'I see America! The lights are burning!' . . . Before I knew what happened I was standing by the rail and the whole world was lit." Oreste Teglia, coming to America in 1916 at 12 years old, said, "The most amazing sight to me was the tall buildings, with their windows lit, just like a fantasyland."[37]

Edward Corsi, later commissioner of immigration at Ellis Island, describes his voyage and entry into America at the age of 11 this way:

> My first impression of the new world will always remain etched in my memory, particularly that hazy October morning when I first saw Ellis Island. The steamer *Florida*, fourteen days out of Naples, filled to capacity with sixteen hundred natives of Italy, had weathered one of the worst storms in our captain's memory; and glad we were, both children and grown-ups, to leave the open sea and come at last through the Narrows into the Bay. My mother, my stepfather, my brother Giuseppe, and my two sisters, Liberta and Helvetia, all of us together, happy that we had come through the storm safely, clustered on the foredeck for fear of separation and looked with wonder on this miraculous land of our dreams . . . Passengers all about us crowded against the rail. Jabbered conversation, sharp cries, laughs and cheers—a steadily rising din filled the air. Mothers and fathers lifted up their babies so that they too could see, off to the left, the Statue of Liberty . . . I looked at the Statue with a sense of bewilderment, half doubting its reality . . . Many older persons among us, burdened with a thousand memories of what they were leaving behind, had been openly weeping.[38]

Not all immigrants saw the Statue of Liberty. At departure ports such as Hamburg, unscrupulous sea captains would agree to take immigrants to America at a low cost. Not knowing one ship from another, immigrants crowded into these often unseaworthy vessels, and they set sail. According to Manny Steen, who emigrated from Ireland in 1925 at age 19, Jewish immigrants from eastern Europe were sometimes tricked by captains who "dumped a load of [these] refugees on the east coast of Scotland during the night in a little seaport. They just dumped them off and said, 'This is America' and they took off . . . The people thought they were in America because they couldn't speak any English."[39]

Arrival

Between 1892 and 1924, the peak years of a worldwide migration, the United States saw approximately 20 million enter, with over 14 million coming through Ellis Island. Ellis Island opened in 1892 and replaced the inadequate and aging Castle Garden, situated at the Battery on the New York City shore, and serving as an immigration center since 1855. Castle Garden had many problems in regard to space and an inadequate inspection process. In 1888, 76 percent of immigrants coming to the United States entered through Castle Garden. As the immigration numbers rose and federal legislation made the inspection process more important and intense, Castle Garden deficiencies became more significant. As one Italian immigrant described it in 1884, "The inside was a big, dark room full of dust, with fingers of light coming down from the ceiling. The room was already crowded with poor people from earlier boats sitting on benches and railings and on the floor. To one side were a few tables where food was being sold."[40] More than eight million immigrants arrived at Castle Garden in the years it was in operation. When the ships came into port, boardinghouse runners immediately besieged the immigrants. These dockside criminals and con men tried to convince the immigrants to come to their boardinghouses, or simply grabbed their luggage and had the immigrant follow them. The resultant charge for these "services" was exorbitant.

Congress and the press often discussed Castle Garden's problems, which included overcrowding, poorly performed medical inspections, disregard for regulatory immigration laws, cheating of immigrants by those who preyed on these newcomers unfamiliar with city ways, and disease concerns. Joseph Pulitzer of the *New York World* made the poor situation at Castle Garden a particular concern, although conditions had improved from the time when the crooks actually came on board to fleece the immigrants. But troubles did not end with the closing of Castle Garden; some of these issues reappeared at Ellis Island. However, the state-run Castle Garden did set some important precedents: medical inspections (even if hastily done), immigrant aid societies to advocate for the immigrants, and the ability to exchange currency and to buy legitimate railroad tickets to travel inland. Castle Garden served as the place where later Ellis Island procedures were tried out and revamped for the new station. Immigration became a federal rather than a state responsibility in 1891, mainly owing to worries over the quality and origins of the immigrants entering and a growing public belief that the federal government could handle the inflow better. Fear that European governments sent their problem people to America inspired more attention to comprehensive examinations. Between 1890 and 1892, when Ellis Island saw the construction of docks and buildings, immigration officials used the relatively small and very cramped Barge Office on the Battery for processing. The federal government's shift into a more regulatory approach to immigration paralleled its other Progressive Era controls in regard to industry and railroads, such as the Interstate Commerce Act of 1887 and the Sherman Antitrust Act of 1890. The government's power expanded in relation to the growing power of industry and the more complex aspects of American life.[41]

Prior to Angel Island's opening, Chinese and other Asian immigrants experienced especially poor conditions. Chinese immigrants coming to San Francisco found themselves in a small, two-story wooden building awaiting inspection. An American missionary to the Chinese, Reverend Ira Condit, wrote of the conditions in 1900: "Merchants, laborers, are all alike penned up, like a flock of sheep, in a wharf-shed, for many days, and often weeks, at their own expense, and are denied all communication with their own people while the investigation of their cases moves its show length along." The commissioner of immigration at that port, F. P. Sargent, soon admitted that the "detention shed should be abolished forthwith. Chinese are human beings and are entitled to humane treatment, and this is something they do not receive under present conditions." The *Chinese World* newspaper in San Francisco wrote in 1910 that "ever since the establishment of this wooden shed at the wharf, the mistreatment of us Chinese confined there was worse than for jailed prisoners . . . There were even some who could not endure the cruel abuse and took their own lives." One other Chinese observer compared the shed to a jail, noting that "the interior is about one hundred feet square.

Oftentimes they put in as many as two hundred human beings . . . The air is impure, the place is crowded." Outsiders could not visit without official authorization, and letters were forbidden. "We were treated like a group of animals, and we were fed on the floor." These sentiments, plus concern over health issues, inspired the construction of the Angel Island facility.[42] Fear of contagious diseases that the immigrants might bring to the mainland partly explains why these stations were located on islands. Angel Island's quarantine station actually opened in 1892, 18 years before Angel Island became the official immigration station.

A total of 3,818 ships arrived at Ellis Island in 1907, the peak year, indicating the enormity of the processing job. As the ship sailed closer to its final destination, state quarantine officials boarded the ship for a final quick examination of its human cargo for any communicable diseases or other health problems that would warrant keeping all the immigrants on board. Customs inspectors also boarded at this time. Quarantine medical officials stopped ships with passengers having cholera or other contagious diseases as defined by law until the disease no longer appeared evident or the sick passengers had been transferred to quarantine hospitals nearby. The quarantine laws did not call for the isolation of those with other health problems such as insanity, scarlet fever, measles, and trachoma. Yet immigration officials delayed some sick immigrants when they disembarked at the pier and transported them to New York hospitals. All this was done before any immigrant went to Ellis Island for processing. Immigration inspectors and doctors from the Marine Hospital Service (later called the Public Health Service) also boarded to perform a perfunctory inspection of the first- and second-class passengers, who were initially not required to go to Ellis Island, and to check the ship manifest to see that all was legitimate. One immigrant aid worker described the doctor's visit in the following way: "As quickly as possible, the little doctor, who was working for the Public Health Service, would climb up and down the ladder on those ships that came in—he worked very, very hard. Sometimes they had to meet a ship at two or three o'clock in the morning."[43] First- and second-class privileges, for individuals who could afford to pay more for the journey, also allowed those who might be rejected to slip into the country.

Booking second-class became a way some immigrants tried to avoid a more stringent Ellis Island inspection if they suspected that they would not pass. Some even paid first-class to avoid detection. Criminals and other undesirables who had the money to pay for a first-class ticket could easily get into the country. In 1906, a passenger who had been deported earlier for medical reasons returned in first-class while his family went via steerage. Unfortunately for him, the inspectors remembered him, and he and his entire family were then deported.[44] On some occasions, the immigration officials intensified their inspection on the first- and second-class passengers. Officials came on board a ship arriving in 1912, put all first- and second-class passengers on a line, and had them respond to numerous questions. Six of these passengers had to go to Ellis Island with the steerage immigrants. But handling first- and second-class passengers in this way caused an uproar of disapproval from the shipping companies and the wealthy, for whom class distinctions took on great importance. The companies received extra money for the privileges that went with these cabins. Walter Mrozowski, arriving from Poland in the early years of the twentieth century, said that "when the boat landed in New York I found there were two classes of people: the poor ones and the ones who looked like they had some money and were dressed that way. I was among those who looked like I had money, so I had no trouble getting off the boat" although "I had only $10 in my pocket." Those individuals considered as higher class maintained their privileged treatment throughout this era, even when commissioners tried to change the class system. As one steamship official noted, "A man in the first-class cabin might consider it almost a joke to be, as he would express it, put with immigrants."[45] The effort to give more than a perfunctory examination to the "better" travelers failed after stirring up so much controversy.

One notable case involved the SS *Massilia*, which came into New York Harbor in 1892 filled with approximately 800 passengers and crew. Two doctors examined the group in less than one hour for various diseases, including "typhus, cholera, plague, yellow fever, smallpox, and leprosy."[46] Obviously, the time spent indicated a cursory exam. The ship had been cleared at the port of departure and then given approval to enter the harbor. Medical personnel and inspectors also screened passengers at Ellis Island, and no contagious health problems appeared among them. But after the immigrants scattered throughout New York, typhus became evident, indicating the failure of the health exam system in this case and raising concerns and even panic about the need for better health inspections. These immigrants had to be gathered up and quarantined at once in what became a series of tragic family events. The building at 5 Essex Street in New York was one of the typhus hotbeds, as some of the *Massilia* passengers settled there. The New York Sanitary Police were ordered to bring the infected to a quarantine hospital on a nearby island, forcibly if necessary, as in the case of Fayer Mermer, a 40-year-old mother of five. She was pulled "kicking and screaming . . . in full view of her husband, children, and neighbors" out of the house. Her two children who were infected survived, but she died after six days. In another situation, the United Hebrew Charities had assigned the Galinsky family, from another ship, to the Essex Street house. Realizing the danger of that house, the parents moved the children to a friend's apartment on Hester Street while they looked for better quarters outside the city. The children had already been infected, and the police, finding out, went to the Hester Street address and took the children to the hospital. Doctors restored the children to health, but 13 other *Massilia* passengers died. Anyone who had been in contact with the ship's passengers had to be removed and quarantined until doctors were certain that they carried no disease. The roundup involved thousands, all sent to the quarantine hospital for examination. Nonetheless, the city averted an epidemic. The threat of individuals with contagious diseases being allowed into America remained a strong fear among the American public and led to a tightening of the medical examinations.

Some immigrants had been inspected three times before entering Ellis Island: once at the train terminal in Europe, once at the departure port, and now on the ship. The final inspection would come on Ellis Island, and this one particularly frightened many who did not want to be turned back at that final point and after all their effort to get to America. As the Ellis Island–bound ship docked at the New York or Hoboken, New Jersey, pier, most immigrants moved to barges that would take them to Ellis Island. At times, the ship had to delay the passengers' debarkation because of overcrowding due to previous ships' arrivals. Angelina Palmiero, from Sicily, remembered her father, who was waiting for the family to arrive, coming alongside the ship in a tugboat. Using a pail, he managed to send up to the ship some bananas he bought on the tug. Angelina said she "didn't know what bananas were. 'Don't eat it like that,'" her father said; "'Take the skin off.'"[47] Those claiming U.S. citizenship went ashore quickly if their papers proved legitimate. However, any individual whose papers did not look correct went on to Ellis Island along with steerage immigrant passengers.

As the immigrants went from the ship to the dock, they experienced a tumultuous time. In one case, as an Italian immigrant woman was getting off the ship holding a child, a deck chair brought from home, and a big pack, thereby slowing the movement off the ship as she obstructed the passageway, one of the crew "dragged her down, tore the chair off her arm, splitting her sleeve as he did so and scrapping the skin off her wrist, and in his rage he broke the chair into a dozen pieces."[48] Crying, the woman moved along but did not complain, indicating both the arrivals' docility and the crews' sometimes brutal treatment.

The Ellis Island immigrants' large numbers produced tense situations for crew, immigration officials, and immigrants as the assembly went to their proper places. Going from the dock to the barge or ferry, immigrants received numbered tags to be placed on their clothes and baggage so that the movement through Ellis Island could be monitored and done in an orderly fashion. The barges could transport hundreds of immigrants for the short voyage to the island. Even this short journey frightened some immigrants, but others were elated that they had arrived in America. Corsi relates,

> During this ride across the bay, as I watched the faces of the people milling about me, I realized that Ellis Island could inspire both hope and fear. Some of the passengers were afraid and obviously dreading the events of the next few hours; others were impatient, anxious to get through the inspection and be off to their destinations . . . each family huddled over its trunks and boxes, suitcases or bundles wrapped in bedding. Some were guarding grimy piles of worn bedding wound about with string or rope or wire. Among the horde of bewildered peasants were some with their pitiful, paltry personal belongings, all they had in the world, tied up in old blue or red bandannas, which they clutched anxiously as they peered over the rail toward the tiny island where their fate would be decided.[49]

Officials only allowed immigrants on these boats; others, including relatives who had come to meet their families, had to take the ferry to the island.

Helen Barth, who worked at Ellis Island on behalf of the Hebrew Immigrant Aid Society from 1914 to 1917, discussed the barge carriers: "The boats that took the immigrants in [from the dock to the island] were not very good boats, but they were large enough to carry hundreds at a time . . . They were flat-bottom boats. The immigrants were very fearful, terribly afraid." Theodore Lubik, arriving in 1913 and later working at Ellis Island, described the process of getting from ship to barge: "They brought you to Ellis Island with that small boat—it might take a couple of hundred or even a thousand people. The regular ship would pull up to the pier, but the little one moved somehow next to the ship and transferred the people over there."[50] Annie Moore, coming from Ireland, was the first immigrant to be accepted into America at the newly opened Ellis Island in 1892.

As sometimes happened, immigrants remained on these crowded barges for hours if the processing line at Ellis Island had slowed as a result of some problem, or if too many immigrants preceded them in line. Whether immigrants would get speedy processing from the ship to the barge to Ellis Island often depended on when the ship or barge arrived. Ships arriving in the middle of the night often had to hold their passengers on board until the morning. Passengers on barges that arrived at noon at Ellis Island would often have to wait until 2 p.m. before processing started, when doctors, inspectors, and other officials returned from lunch. As Brandenburg relates, while waiting on the barge, "children cried, mothers strove to hush them, the musically inclined sang or played, and then the sun went down while we waited and still waited."[51] Nonetheless, immigrants received food on the barge while they waited. The food consisted of whatever was available in the kitchen at that time, including milk, coffee, sardines, herring, and bread.

On the West Coast, ships arriving in San Francisco sent immigrants, except for those in first or second class or with clearly correct papers, by ferry to Angel Island as of 1910. The others were allowed to enter the United States. Class distinctions for quarantined individuals, as on ship, remained. First- and second-class passengers lived in separate barrack areas so that they would not come into contact with steerage arrivals. One major difference at this immigration station was that the Chinese were singled out from other Asians, and whites also were split from the others. The quarantine station, built prior to the Angel Island immigration facility, had barracks just for Chinese and just for Japanese quarantined arrivals. The process for those suspected of having a disease was that "each morning and evening the steerage passengers lined up, and received an inspection by one of the medical officers to make sure there were no new outbreaks of the disease and to check for escapes. Every morning the barracks were fumigated . . . and then flushed out with salt water." Even after Angel Island opened, the quarantine area was not kept well. In 1912, the *San Francisco Call* wrote that "the Chinese barracks . . . is now unfit for human habitation."[52]

Ellis Island, a small three-acre island in New York Harbor, went through various transformations and names. The Lenni Lenape tribe (also known as the Delaware tribe) referred to the island as Gull Island. For the Dutch and

English, it was first known as Little Oyster Island owing to the oyster beds available there. Since pirates were routinely executed there in the early nineteenth century, New Yorkers called it Gibbet Island (after the instrument used to hang them). Although known by some other names as well, the island acquired its permanent name in the eighteenth century from Samuel Ellis, who owned the property. After New York State bought the island in 1808, it reassigned control to the federal government, which built a new fort and used the island as a munitions depot for the city's protection. With immigration increasing in the late nineteenth century and the extensive problems associated with the station at Castle Garden, the federal government authorized the construction of the main immigrant-receiving station at the island, so designated in 1890 by President Benjamin Harrison. As immigrants approached Ellis Island in the late nineteenth century, they saw one main wooden building of two stories, which incrementally increased to 41 buildings that included dorms, a kitchen, a power house, a carpenter shop, a ferry house, a mental ward, administration buildings for the hospitals, recreation halls, and various other office spaces.

A devastating fire in 1897 destroyed the Ellis Island structures and closed the processing center for over three years. Ellis Island buildings reappeared better than before, rebuilt using brick materials. The Ellis Island processing center eventually spread over three adjacent islands, two of which were manmade with landfills. Since the initial plans for the new station were inadequate, facilities had to be expanded a number of times. Immigration officials based their calculations for a new station on the lower immigration totals of the 1890s, when the country was suffering through a depression. Predictions suggested fewer immigrants in the future, not more. The numbers, however, rapidly increased over the next 20 years. Along with the tightening of qualifications to enter the country, the sense of the commissioner-general of immigration in 1897 was that "I do not apprehend that immigration will ever reach the volume of past years, notwithstanding the most prosperous conditions in our country."[53] Unexpected immigrant waves pushed into Ellis Island in the next few years.

During construction of new Ellis Island facilities, immigrants again went to the Barge Office building on the New York dock, where the U.S. Customs Bureau had been housed, until the new structures reopened for processing in 1900. Detained immigrants were placed on a ship in New York Harbor and in two houses near the Barge Office. Nearby hospitals or the detention ship

Figure 1. How Ellis Island looked in 1905 as immigrants approached the island on barges after disembarking at the New York port. Courtesy of Library of Congress, LC-USZ62-37784.

received sick individuals. The hospital situation was not adequate even after the new Ellis Island hospital opened. Overcrowding meant sending ill immigrants to other hospitals and led to escapes and the removal of immigrants from Ellis Island official supervision. Even at this point with rebuilding taking place, most immigrants coming to the United States went through the New York port. Of those arriving in 1899 with a contagious disease and deported, 95 percent were excluded at the New York station. More funds went to the Ellis Island center than to any other entry point.

The intent of the rebuilt Ellis Island, as noted in *Harper's Weekly*, was to construct fireproof buildings "which would keep immigrants free from all outside interference until discharged, while affording means for relatives and friends to communicate with them at the proper time."[54] The new main structure, although similar in square feet to its predecessor, was a stunning edifice: built with red brick over a steel frame with four high copper overlaid towers, it had eagles and shields on the large arches over the windows. The rebuilt structure had expanded space for offices, dining rooms, inspection and interrogation rooms, areas for showering, and a recreational roof section.[55] Outside the front entrance was a canopy (built in 1903) to protect the immigrants from the weather while they waited. The entry floor housed an area for baggage, railroad tickets and other offices, a waiting room for those traveling further inland, and places to buy food. The main building, constructed not just to make the processing more efficient but to inspire wonder in America's new arrivals, became the symbol of Ellis Island. The Great Hall or Registry Room on the second floor, where the main inspections would take place, had been designed in a similar inspirational fashion: a high tiled ceiling over a two-story room, with chandeliers and globes (1917–1918) hanging from the ceiling. Large windows provided lighting from the outside. The floor was tiled like the ceiling. Around the room, and as part of the third level, was a balcony with iron rails and tiled floor, with electric lights (1911) just under the railing.[56] The Great Hall, decorated with large American flags as of 1914, was divided into sections bounded by iron railings (later benches), forcing the immigrants into single-file lines. A staircase stood in the center of the hall (later replaced by one on the east side) bringing arrivals up from the first floor. Offices were on the mezzanine level. Along with the Great Hall, the second floor had sections for detention, inspection, medical examination, a laboratory, offices, and waiting. The iron railings in the Great Hall created the strongest memory for most immigrants and are seen in many photos of that period. These railings forced the immigrants into distinct lines and prevented chaos among the large number of people waiting to be inspected.

Ellis Island eventually consisted of 27.5 acres across its three islands. Using dirt and rocks from various sources, including the digging of the New York subway, Ellis Island took on its modern form. The main island, where the largest building stood, housed the Great Hall inspection area. This island also contained buildings for baggage and dormitory space, laundry and kitchen facilities, a dining area, an incinerator, a power house, a bakery, and carpentry areas. Between islands one and two stood the Ferry House and dock. Island two had a laundry and linen exchange building, which also contained an autopsy room and mortuary (also referred to as the hospital outbuilding) and hospital areas including offices and a mental ward. In the passageway connecting islands two and three were the recreation buildings.

Passageways also connected buildings on the islands. The third island housed the power equipment, administration and staff buildings, medical wards for contagious diseases, and a laundry. Spread over islands two and three were over 30 places for hospital work.[57]

The new Ellis Island station received positive press coverage when it reopened in 1900. The *New York Tribune* stated that "the impression of the way things are done in the United States made upon the immigrant who arrived to-day will be a more favorable one than that made upon his brother who arrived here a week ago. He will enter this country by the gateway of the new immigration station on Ellis Island, instead of the grimy, gloomy Barge Office—more suggestive of an inclosure [*sic*] for animals than a receiving station for prospective citizens of the United States." The *Architectural Record* said that the station met the needs of "'both a hospice and a hospital,' and also essentially that of a railroad station, [and] the requirement of landing, collecting, and distributing great and sudden crowds with a minimum of confusion and delay." The *Record* went on to comment that "'the general composition of the central building, the distribution of the masses and the treatment of them' were 'thoroughly admirable.'"[58]

However, space for inspections, hospitalization, baggage, and sleeping was always a problem, and the facilities expanded over the years to meet the significant daily demands. Initially the island station had been constructed to process 500,000 immigrants per year, but in peak years the numbers soared beyond that figure. Space for detainees, as more immigrants were so categorized, became a particular problem. Over the years, some improvements were made as space was increased and used more efficiently. Ellis Island, along with other immigration stations, was meant to pay for itself through a head tax of $4.00 charged to each immigrant to enter the United States, included as part of the steamship ticket price. But the government absorbed these funds and only gave back a small percentage to run the immigration stations. As a result, although the federal government earned more funds from the immigration trade than they spent, the immigration process remained consistently underfunded.

Angel Island, which an early Spanish explorer named, also had an administration building, a hospital, a detention center, storage buildings, a power plant, and staff housing. The administration building area accommodated immigrant inspections. As described in a 1907 *San Francisco Chronicle* article as the station was being completed, "It contains separate dining rooms for Europeans, Chinese and Japanese, for employees, visitors and officers, a baggage room, offices of the custom inspector, board of inquiry, Chinese Inspector, Commissioner of Immigration . . . as well as Chinese and Japanese detention departments." The Europeans had sleeping quarters in the administration building, while the Chinese and Japanese each had separate dormitories in another building. However, the facilities were subpar, as even the commissioner-general of immigration, W. W. Husband, admitted in 1922. He said that "the plant has practically nothing to commend it. It is made of a conglomeration of ramshackle buildings which are nothing but firetraps. They are illy [*sic*] arranged and inconvenient. The sanitary arrangements are awful. If a private individual had such an establishment he would be arrested by the local health authorities."[59] Both before and after the Angel Island facility was built, the San Francisco Chinese community opposed placing immigrants on this inhospitable island. And the Chinese were correct in protesting, for the island provided poor conditions for Chinese detainees, and the percentage rejected swelled once the island station was opened. The main Chinese organization, the Chinese Six Companies, considered the conditions so bad that they urged immigrants to bypass Angel Island and go elsewhere to enter the United States. Many individuals, including Husband, wanted to abandon the island and shift the immigrant station to the mainland. Immigration officials finally made this move in 1940. The island also had two military bases and a quarantine station built earlier.

As difficult as the journey and Ellis Island experience would be for many entrants, it was relatively welcoming compared to that of Asian immigrants, especially Chinese, arriving at Angel Island. The intent at Ellis Island was to admit immigrants while checking them carefully; at Angel Island, the clear intent was to enforce the Chinese exclusion laws and refuse entry, except for certain individuals who were "officials, merchants, teachers, students, and travelers for curiosity or pleasure" or those born in the United States. Later, exclusion became almost complete for all Chinese. Others, such as those from South Asia, would also have a difficult time. In 1910 at Angel Island, Asians were summarily excluded on the basis of possibly becoming a public charge, yet Russians, who could easily have been excluded for the same reason, were admitted. Europeans arriving at Angel Island would be treated similarly to those arriving at Ellis Island. Generally they would be allowed entry within a brief time. At Ellis Island, inspectors formally based entry on mental and physical health and a desire and willingness to work. The San Francisco and later Angel Island stations' criteria assumed that the Asian, and particularly Chinese, immigrant was unacceptable, and therefore these people had to show why admittance was their right. As a result, Chinese rejections were high. In the fiscal years of 1903–1905, even those immigrants who were exempt from the exclusion laws had a 25 percent rejection rate. From 1901 to 1910, before the island station opened, about 560 Chinese faced deportation each year. Chinese American citizens had difficulty reentering the United States and had to have extensive paperwork to prove their case. Yet, although at least 100,000 Chinese dealt with detention at Angel Island in the period from 1910 to 1940, 178,000 (mostly arriving at San Francisco and the island) were allowed entry "as new immigrants, returning residents, and U.S. citizens." Some entered the United States from easier entry points at the Mexican or Canadian border.[60] The exclusion laws did not keep most Chinese out of the country. One important factor is that these laws and the general effort to reject Chinese immigrants led to the use by a large majority of Chinese arrivals of false papers as a way of securing entry. These papers could claim that the immigrant was a merchant or part of another exempt group, was born in the United States, or was a child of those exempt or born in America. The last category produced the phenomenon of "paper sons."

The obliteration of records in the 1906 San Francisco earthquake and fire made it easy to claim either native-born status or a child of exempt or U.S.-born individuals. Chinese new arrivals could falsely say they had more children than existed and then market the extra child classifications to others. As one paper son immigrant explained, "You tell the immigration officer, 'I have been in China three years, I have three sons, these are their birthdays, the names and so forth.'" Then either their real sons would come over, or papers were purchased by those who wanted to emigrate from China. "There's always lots of buyers ready to pay. You try to sell to your own village, or a similar last name."[61] A migration system was therefore established that permitted many illegal Chinese immigrants to be classified as legal entries during this early period and beyond. Real and fake family members could then bring in their relatives and thereby thwart the exclusion laws.

At times, for example, in the World War I years, the U.S. armed forces also used Ellis and Angel Islands for military matters. During those war years, the army and navy took control of many of Ellis Island's buildings. The hospitals cared for wounded American soldiers, forcing immigration officials to move hospitalized immigrants to other medical facilities in New York. Some enemy aliens were housed on the island as well. The war's main event for Ellis Island was the Black Tom explosion in 1916. German saboteurs caused a massive explosion of a munitions area close to the island, which damaged some buildings, including the main structure. The island returned to immigration inspection in 1919, with the end of the war, and fairly quickly saw a large-scale postwar immigration emerge.

Frightened, awestruck, invigorated, and confused by all that they saw and experienced on their arrival day, immigrants now started the main inspection process. A whirlwind awaited them. As one Ellis Island observer noted, "Hour after hour, ship load after ship load, day after day, the stream of human beings with its kaleidoscopic variations was then hurried along through Ellis Island by the equivalent of 'step lively' in every language of the earth."[62] Still, as another observer wrote, "It is a busy island. Yet in all the rushing hurry and seeming confusion of a full day, in all the babel of language, the excitement and fright and wonder of the thousands of newly-landed, and in all the manifold and endless details that make up the immigration plant, there is system, silent, watchful, swift, efficient."[63] Steiner in 1905 spoke clearly of what to expect: "Let no one believe that landing on the shores of 'The land of the free and the home of the brave' is a pleasant experience. It is a hard, harsh fact, surrounded by the grinding machinery of the law, which sifts, picks, and chooses; admitting the fit and excluding the weak and helpless."[64] It was an industrial processing similar to the manufacture of goods in America's new mechanized factories.

2 How Immigrants Were Processed

THE IMMIGRANT was sent into a separate room, and the Public Health doctor asked the new arrival an odd question: would he throw over a loaf of bread or a gold bar if he was on a small boat adrift in the ocean? The wrong answer could mark the immigrant (referred to as aliens at that time) as mentally deficient and excluded from entry into the United States. The question, one of many the immigrants were asked after a long and exhausting journey from the Old World, often confused them. What did questions such as this mean, and how did the examination process work?

Inspection

Most Ellis Island immigrants passed through the entire inspection process within five hours, but some were detained for various reasons. For example, in 1907, the peak immigration year, of the 1,004,756 immigrants who arrived, 195,540 were detained. Detentions were usually short, with the majority of detainees waiting for relatives or funds before release, as were 121,737 in that year. Those detained longer included 64,510 who eventually had to appear before a special inquiry board for more serious concerns and 9,293 confined to hospitals. Ultimately, 6,752 deportations occurred for various issues. Although most detainees eventually secured admittance, they had to endure intensive physical and mental examinations, hospitalization, and perhaps appeals. For cabin passengers (first and second class) in the 1906/1907 fiscal year, out of 143,120 arrivals, 5,024 faced detention, with 2,988 of this group held for special inquiry and 288 finally deported. In 1911, the year with the highest percentage of arrivals deported, statistics show around 637,000 admitted and about 13,000 deported, or roughly 2 percent. In 1914, records indicate 878,052 admitted, with 175,580 detained and eventually 16,588 deported.[1] During the period from 1892 to 1910, the main reason for exclusion was "likely to become a public charge," with the second cause being contract labor (immigrants contracted to come to America to engage in labor that might compete with American workers). However, in the 1911–1920 period, while the public charge issue remained prominent, mental and physical factors assumed second place. Other reasons in both periods included immorality, criminal behavior, illiteracy (after 1917), subversive or anarchist activity (after 1903), and illegal entry (e.g., not having any documents for entry).[2] Although those deported always remained a relatively low percentage of arrivals, they still included many thousands of individuals who often had to return without any relatives left in the old country, without funds, or to situations dangerous to their lives.

At Angel Island, an estimated 340,000 immigrants arrived in the years from 1910 to 1940, after which the station was closed. Out of that number, and although estimates vary, at least 100,000 experienced detention.[3] The large detainee numbers illustrate the harshness of the exclusion laws and the determined efforts not to let too many Chinese or other Asians into the United States. The Chinese arriving before and after Angel Island opened realized a significantly higher rejection rate than at Ellis Island for all immigrants. Chinese arriving through Ellis Island were also singled out for special attention.

At Ellis Island, if one family member was rejected, or hospitalized, or delayed in some other manner, other family members faced an emotional decision of what to do. As they entered the processing system, immigrants did not know what their fate would be, causing much trepidation as they moved along the inspection line. Even for those who passed through quickly, this day could be very unpleasant. Louis Adamic, arriving in 1913, said, "The day I spent on Ellis Island was an eternity. Rumors were current among immigrants of several nationalities that some of us would be refused admittance into the United States and sent back to Europe. For several hours I was in a

Figure 2. A crowd of immigrants waiting for their entry into the main building at Ellis Island for the all-important examinations. What were they thinking at this time as they stood outside America's Door? Courtesy of Library of Congress, LC-B201-5202-13.

cold sweat on this account, although, so far as I knew, all my papers were in order." Then he started worrying about catching some disease: "I had heard that several hundred sick immigrants were quarantined on the island." Stephen Graham, arriving from England in 1913, said, "It was the hardest day since leaving Europe and home . . . we were driven in herds from one place to another, ranged into single files, passed in review before doctors, poked in the eyes by the eye-inspectors, cross-questioned by the pocket-inspectors, vice detectives, and blue-book compilers."[4]

For others, a worse experience occurred. For example, Doukenie Papandreos, arriving in 1919 at age 15, was terrified as she waited for the examination. Facing a Public Health Service doctor in military uniform, whom many immigrants assumed was a soldier, made them more afraid given their Old World experiences with government and military officials. As she said, "Next to me was an Italian woman with three children, and one of the children sick . . . The child was coughing. The mother was holding the child and singing. All of a sudden, a doctor and two nurses took the child away. The mother couldn't speak English. And they were talking to her in English. They were saying that the child had to go to the hospital. And they took the child from her arms, and the mother was crying," not understanding what was happening.

As Papandreos waited over the next few days unaware of her own fate, she remembered thinking, "I couldn't enjoy nothing. I was afraid they were going to send me back. And I was dreaming that if they try to send me back, I'm going to fall into the river and die. I couldn't go back."[5] Edward Steiner observed that a Polish woman near him "suddenly became aware that she has one less child clinging to her skirts, and she implores me with agonizing cries, to bring it back to her. In a strange world, at the very entrance to what is to be her new home, without the protection of her husband, without any knowledge of the English language, and with no one taking the trouble to explain to her the reason, the child was snatched from her side. Somewhere it is bitterly crying for its mother, and each is unconscious of the other's fate."[6] Even minor events, which immigrants misunderstood, could increase anxiety. Catherine Bolinski, who came to America in the early 1920s as a child from Poland, said that when she came before the doctors, she "wasn't unbuttoning fast enough, so they shoved me out of sight. My mother got scared; she thought they were going to send me back." Sir Auckland Geddes, the British ambassador to the United States, toured Ellis Island in 1922 and in his report to his government noted the immigrants' misunderstanding of normal procedures: during the medical exam, as men and women were separated and "not understanding what is happening, strange and nervous, some of the wretched immigrants believe that they are being separated for ever." A husband and wife placed into separate examination rooms, even for a short time, leads on occasion, as Geddes was told, "to pathetic scenes."[7] For the Chinese at Angel Island, men and women, husbands and wives were kept apart, although the majority of Chinese immigrants were men.

Frank Martocci, an Ellis Island inspector and interpreter in 1907, when over one million immigrants arrived (including 21,755 in one day on May 2), describes well the overwhelming crowd of people and the inspectors' efficiency:

> To make things run fairly smoothly in that mixed crowd of poor, bewildered immigrants, we would tag them with numbers corresponding to numbers on their manifests, after they had been landed from the barges and taken into the building. Here, in the main building, they were lined up—a motley crowd in colorful costumes, all ill at ease and wondering what was to happen

> to them . . . From nine o'clock in the morning to nine in the evening, we were continuously examining aliens . . . I thought it was a stream that would never end. Every twenty-four hours from three to five thousand people came before us, and I myself examined four to five hundred a day. We were simply swamped by that human tide.[8]

Emanuel Steen, a 19-year-old immigrant arriving in 1925, recalled,

> That day there must have been three, four ships. Maybe five, six thousand people. Jammed! . . . Hot as a pistol and I'm wearing my long johns and a heavy Irish tweed suit . . . Immigration officials slammed a tag on you with your name, address, country of origin, etc. Everybody was tagged. They didn't ask you whether you spoke English or not. They took your papers, and they tagged you. They checked your bag. Then they pushed you and they'd point, because they didn't know if you spoke English or not. Understaffed. Overcrowded. Jammed. And the place was the noisiest, and the languages, and the smell. Foul.[9]

At every stage where immigrants needed an interpreter, officials provided one. By 1911, interpreters were available in 37 languages from Arabic to Yiddish, although not all indicated fluency in both spoken and written communication. Immigration officials urged interpreters to familiarize themselves with more than one language. After 1914, interpreters were required to know minimally two of the following languages: Italian, Polish, Yiddish, German, Greek, Russian, Croatian, Slovenian, Lithuanian, Ruthenian, and Hungarian. Immigrants interacting with interpreters and other Ellis Island staff experienced mixed relations. Some immigrants found the workers helpful, as when they allowed people who could not read in any language to pass the literacy exam; others had significant problems, as did Ida Mouradjian, an Armenian woman arriving in 1922 and remaining at the island for more than three weeks, longer than most. "We were pushed around . . . [The staff] were a bunch of patronage job holders, who were ignorant. What's more, they didn't have hearts, they didn't have minds, they had no education. They were very crude. Many were foreigners, who delighted in the fact that they could lord over the new entries, the new immigrants. They had accents as thick as molasses, every kind of accent, but they acted the way small people become because they had a little power. They pushed everybody around, actually, literally pushed."[10]

Figure 3. Immigrants in the Great Hall Registry Room. After successfully completing the line medical examination, immigrants were moved to this part of the hall in anticipation of the next step: questioning by immigration inspectors. Many immigrants later remembered the maze of iron handrails. Courtesy of Photography Collection, Miriam and Ira D. Wallach Division of Art, Prints and Photographs, The New York Public Library, Astor, Lenox and Tilden Foundations.

In the main building, officials moved the immigrants into lines while keeping people from each ship separated. Immigrants walked up the staircase, carrying some luggage, to the Great Hall, and the medical inspection began. The exam could take minutes if the immigrant looked and acted healthy, but that was not always the case. The doctors of the Marine Hospital Service, later called Public Health Service, observed them at every point, looking for signs of weakness, disability, poor eyesight, lack of balance, and general instability. Even the manner in which the immigrants carried their baggage was of great interest, which Dr. Victor Safford explained could indicate maladies such as a heart condition; problems with shoulders, elbows, and wrists; postural defects; hernias; and weakness. As Dr. Alfred C. Reed describes the procedure in 1912, the doctors would watch how immigrants walked and how they looked. Someone who had trouble adhering to the line and looked at the floor all the time might have vision problems. Immigrants following the line had to turn right at a certain point after facing the doctor so that he would see the immigrants face-forward and then from the side. In this way, using just observation, the doctor "notes the gait, attitude . . . presence of flat feet, lameness, stiffness at ankle, knee, or hip, malformations of the body; observes the neck for goiter, muscular development, scars, enlarged glands, texture of skin . . . abnormalities of the features, eruptions, scars, paralysis, expressions," and in turning the officer could also look at the ears and get a side view of the entire body. The doctor observed the immigrant carefully trying to determine if anything seemed out of place, including mental/emotional issues. If mental abilities or health seemed suspect, the doctor, using an interpreter, asked a few brief but pertinent questions. Any mental concern would be pursued further if the immigrant showed agitation, oddity, nervousness, crying, apathy, particular sadness as indicated on the alien's face, sloppiness, nail biting, indications of alcohol abuse, confusion, or even unusual tranquility. Children older than 2 years, being carried by their mothers, had to show that they could walk. Also children were spoken to in order to see if they could speak and hear.[11]

Immigrants were spaced up to 15 feet apart as they walked to the next medical officer, who was about 30 feet from the first. Moving away toward the second examiner, the doctor could secure a rear view and spot any spinal or similar problems. Observation was a key element in quickly judging the immigrant's medical condition. Those arrivals appearing to be hiding a medical condition were stopped and looked at more closely. Somebody with a coat covering an arm or carrying a child of walking age brought immediate suspicion. As Dr. Eugene H. Mullan noted as a medical inspector in 1917, misgivings would also be directed at someone with a high collar who might be concealing some neck condition or an individual trying to avoid inspection of their hands owing to missing fingers or paralysis. Officials pulled immigrants with any hint of a physical or mental defect off the line, put them in a cage-like detention area, and then sent them to a gender-specific examining room for further study. The line doctors had already marked the suspect immigrant's clothes on the right shoulder with chalk indicating what the defect might be. For example, those with an "X" indicated a possible mental issue;

an "X" circled meant an unambiguous mental concern. But how did doctors primarily determine who should be initially marked with an "X" and taken for further examination? And how could a doctor classify someone as an idiot, for example, based on mere observation? Dr. Mullan explained this aspect of the inspections in 1917: "Many inattentive and stupid-looking aliens are questioned by the medical officer in the various languages as to their age, destination, and nationality. Often simple questions in addition and multiplication are propounded. Should the immigrant appear stupid and inattentive to such an extent that mental defect is suspected, an X is made on his coat." Dr. C. P. Knight said that the following were possible physical signs of an idiot: defects "ranging from 'low receding forehead' to the size of a face out of proportion [to] the size of the head, to deformed or twisted ears, to excessively deep eye sockets created by a protruding brow. Idiots drooled, and were often apathetic or overly excited. 'The expression is stupid, the eyes dull, the speech defective, the tongue swollen and protruding, while the limbs are short and bent and the skin is thick, sallow and greasy.'"[12] Immigrants who looked odd or wore clothing that seemed out of place were detained. Doctors questioned elderly arrivals closely for evidence of senility. Ethnic stereotypes played a role in determining whether an "X" would be chalked on a person. Dr. Mullan commented that an emotional Italian would be considered normal, but one who behaved with the "solidity and indifference" of Polish or Russian immigrants would be suspect for mental issues. The same would be true of other groups who behaved contrary to their stereotype. English immigrants acting like an Irishman or a Jewish arrival would instigate concerns about their sanity.[13]

Every impairment had a letter, and the letters stood for a particular body part: for example, "B" for back, "H" for heart, "K" for hernia, "L" for lameness, "N" for neck; and it continued for scalp ("Sc"), senility ("S"), and other ailments. Dr. Mullen said that "the words hands, measles, nails, skin, temperature, vision, voice, which are often used, are written out in full."[14]

Some immigrants tried to wipe off the chalk mark; others did not know what it meant and did not want to do something wrong. Beatrice Cohen Conan from Greece recalls the family memory that when her mother arrived in 1903, she received a chalk mark due to her eyes. The father, distraught at the thought of his wife being sent back, asked, "'What could I do?' So, whoever was there in charge said, 'Go over to her. Erase the chalk mark that's on the lapel or on her back, and bring her over to this side and just walk out as though nobody ever put a chalk mark on her.' And he did exactly that."[15] The chalk mark did not necessarily mean that rejection would follow, since 15–20 percent of immigrants were so marked in 1917, but far fewer were rejected. But the whole process did cause much concern among the new arrivals.

The placing of a mark could be traumatic for the immigrant. Dr. Milton Foster commented in 1915, "Not realizing that they are sick, they cannot understand by what stroke of scurvy fortune they have been selected from among all the others and forbidden to enter the Promised Land. The more excitable burst into tears, wring their hands, and protest loudly against the great and unexpected injustice. It is useless to try to calm or reassure them."[16]

The next doctor, the so-called eye man, was there for one purpose: to look at the eyes for various eye diseases, but particularly trachoma, a contagious and dreaded eye disease that could result in blindness and was immediate cause for rejection (this disease can be cured easily today). Immigrants worried the most about this examination since it was said to hurt and was a frightening procedure. The doctors used a buttonhook or their fingers to turn the eyelid inside out, scanning for sores that would indicate trachoma. Fiorello La Guardia, an interpreter at Ellis Island in 1907 and later mayor of New York, commented that "sometimes if it was a young child who suffered from trachoma, one of the parents had to return to the native country with the rejected member of the family. When they learned their fate, they were stunned. They had never felt ill. They had never heard the word trachoma. They could see all right, and they had no homes to return to."[17] One Italian mother traveling in 1903 with her infant who she suspected had eye problems fed the child as much as possible before leaving the ship "so that the doctor should pass it without examining it, as she was prepared to protest against its being waked up."[18] One description of the dreaded eye exam follows: the doctor "stands directly in the path of the immigrant holding a little stick in his hand. By a quick movement and the force of his own compelling gaze, he catches the eyes of his subject and holds them. You can see the immigrant stop short, lift his head with a quick jerk, and open his eyes very wide. The inspector reaches with a swift movement, catches the eyelash with his thumb and finger, turns it back, and peers under it." President Theodore Roosevelt visited Ellis Island and, disturbed by how the doctors conducted this exam, wrote to the Public Health Service that "I was struck by the way in which the doctors made the examinations with dirty hands and no pretense to clean their instruments, so that it would seem to me that these examinations so conducted would themselves be a fruitful source of carrying infection from diseased to healthy persons."[19]

At this exam, doctors also handed immigrants identification cards, which the immigrants naturally looked at to see what was written. This response was expected, and doctors watched to see if the immigrants squinted or seemed to have any trouble seeing the small print—an unobtrusive way of checking for poor eyesight.

Immigrants not chalked or put into a pen moved along without the doctors saying whether they would be accepted. Doctors did not answer questions regarding entry, which led to further anxiety. The immigration inspectors, not the Public Health medical officers, made final decisions, and emphasis was on keeping the immigrants moving as quickly as possible. Those detained received a medical certificate and went on for further examination. Sometimes the examination would go quickly, the issue resolved, and the immigrant sent on to the immigration inspectors. If the immigrant required more complex testing, further delay occurred. Any medical problem, for example, a bad cold, bloodshot eyes, or a runny nose, would prolong the immigrant's stay on the island. Samuel Rexsite, a Jewish immigrant in 1920 from Poland, who caught a cold on board the ship, was detained at Ellis Island while his father was accepted. He "cried and begged [the doctor] to be let in," but had to stay a few days more until the cold subsided.[20]

Privacy did not exist even if an immigrant went for further examination, and this troubled the newcomers. Emanuel Steen describes his experience in the following way:

> I think, frankly, the worst memory I have of Ellis Island was the physical because the doctors were seated at a long table with a basin full of potassium chloride, and you had to stand in front of them and they'd ask you to reveal yourself . . . Right there in front of everyone, I mean it wasn't private! You were standing there. And the women had to open their blouse. This was terrible . . . I was embarrassed as hell . . . I had to open my trousers and fly, and they checked me for venereal disease or hernia or whatever they were looking for.[21]

Women doctors, with the first one put on staff in 1913, examined the female patients, but also not in privacy. Adele Sinko, a 17-year-old Austrian immigrant arriving after World War I, remembered years later that the exam "was so embarrassing for me. I wasn't even twenty-one, very bashful, and

Figure 4. Public Health doctors in 1913 examining the eyes of immigrants. This trachoma test was the most feared. Not only might it be painful, but immigrants could be rejected for an ailment of which they had never heard or felt any symptoms. Courtesy of Library of Congress, LC-USZ62-7386.

there were these big kids running around, but you had to do it. The examination was done by women, but the kids were there. That I resented, when you had to strip to the waistline."[22] Enid Griffiths Jones, arriving in 1923 at age 10 from Wales, remarked on how embarrassed her mother was when the doctors told her to strip. "And my mother had never, ever undressed in front of us. In those days nobody ever would."[23] The mother was mortified but had to comply with the doctors' orders. For those whose detention led to a hospital stay, it was particularly upsetting if the detained immigrant was a child.

Mothers could visit the child on the next day and only during the specified visiting hour.

Three doctors had to sign a medical certificate noting the diagnosis but could not reject the immigrant. Only the immigration inspectors or the Boards of Special Inquiry could do so. In fact, as U.S. Public Health Service doctor Grover Kempf stated in 1912, "I never heard any of the medical officers discuss immigration laws. That was something that was not in our line and there was no indication of the need to discuss these laws."[24]

As immigration laws became enacted over the years, immigrants might sometimes fall into new categories that required medical personnel and immigrant inspectors to provide special treatment, look for the latest specific excludable issue, or ask additional questions. Each inspection stage thereby provoked anxiety since the immigrants could not always be sure what the official wanted as an answer. If they answered incorrectly or if any discrepancies were indicated between the information the inspector had and what the immigrant said, it would result in detention or rejection.

A woman traveling alone dealt with specific questions regarding destination and whether her husband planned to meet her. The inspectors expressed concern about allowing a woman into a big city alone without some male protection, or unease that the woman might be a prostitute. As Stephen Graham, a British author who traveled with the steerage immigrants in 1913, relates, "America is extremely solicitous about the welfare of women, especially of poor, unmarried women who come to her shores. So many women fall into the clutches of evil directly [after] they land in the New World. The authorities generally refuse to admit a poor friendless girl, though there is great demand for female labour all over the United States, and it is easy to get a place and earn a living."[25] Married women had to have their husbands or another immediate relative come to Ellis Island to pick them up and were detained in the interim. In all cases, relatives arriving to escort immigrants off the island had their identities checked for verification. Any discrepancies led to further detention. A 1907 law excluded minors under age 16 traveling without one or both of their parents.

The most confusing and difficult inspector's question was whether the immigrants already had a job waiting for them in America. According to the provisions of the contract labor laws, which labor unions supported to protect their members, immigrants brought into America as part of a contract to work at a particular job were prohibited from entering. This provision attempted to safeguard American jobs and wages. Special contract labor inspectors determined the acceptability of an immigrant. Individual immigrants did not know how to answer this question. Wouldn't it be good to say you had work waiting for you, especially given the concerns evidenced by other questions on whether an immigrant would become a public charge? This was a trick question, and many did not answer correctly: from 1892 to 1920, 34,200 immigrants were rejected for violating these laws, and this category bore one of the highest rejection numbers.[26] Officials also suspected others on the line going to the same destination of being contract laborers. As Frank Martocci, the inspector and Italian interpreter, noted, "It sometimes happened that one member of such a group would produce a letter from a friend or relative within the United States to prove that work had been promised him here. He would willingly sign an affidavit of this, thereby leading not only to his own deportation, but also to that of the entire group."[27] Immigrants eventually learned what to say. The correct answer was that they had a good possibility of a job or that a family member had promised that they could find them a job. Those suspected of being contract laborers received detention cards marked with the letters "U.C." (Under Contract). Detention for those individuals meant that a contract labor inspector would question them further.

In 1917, after years of failure, Congress passed a literacy test in an immigration act over President Woodrow Wilson's veto. The new law required that immigrants over the age of 16 be able to read a passage of up to 40 words in any language in order to be admitted. The Bible was the source for the passages. The test failed to satisfy the restrictionists' desire to limit immigration for southern and eastern Europeans. And as the commissioner of immigration in 1920–1921 related, "We have managed to pass laws bearing no relationship to our needs, such as the literacy test, and then, to make matters worse, their application is made so inhumane and cruel as it is possible to imagine." The test favored those who could read, such as literate criminals, but could result in excluding workers that America needed.[28] The test, when it was first proposed in the 1890s, aimed at class, not race/nationality groups. The test's impulse was directed at admitting those from class segments that were educated and rejecting the poor and uneducated. By the time it passed in 1917, it was clearly directed at eastern and southern Europeans, particularly Jews and Italians, but it failed as a result of increases in literacy rates in all parts of Europe. Exclusion for this reason could not be applied if the immigrant was fleeing religious persecution. Pro-immigration elements fought the law's passage because illiteracy upon entry proved little of an immigrant's potential in America. Chinese who professed to be American citizens had been given a spoken test years earlier to determine English ability, a test Europeans stating U.S. citizenship did not have to take.

Mental Testing

The reasons for exclusion for those detained revolved around a few issues. Although considering the number of people who came through Ellis Island, relatively few were excluded for insanity; still, from 1892 to the end of 1931, 2,012 were denied entry based on this exclusion. Those classified and rejected as idiots from 1892 to 1931 numbered 395, and those rejected as imbeciles from 1908 to 1931 added up to 542.[29] In 1911, 209 mental defectives were detained, 45 percent as feebleminded and 33 percent as insane. For loathsome and contagious diseases that year, of the 1,361 cases, 85 percent were for trachoma. The 1882 immigration law had included as an excludable factor those labeled as lunatics and idiots but left the definition of these terms vague. A 1903 immigration law denied entry to epileptics, insane persons, professional beggars, and idiots and described what would be considered insanity.

This category included such factors as delusions, continuous despair, murderous propensities, or confusion about what is right and wrong to do. A 1907 law added imbeciles and feebleminded persons, and a 1917 law expanded the denied category to constitutional psychopathic inferiority, chronic alcoholism, and mentally defective. Differences between those labeled as idiots, imbeciles, or morons (a new term) related to their perceived mental age determined by intelligence tests: under 3 years, between 3 and 7 years, and between 8 and 12 years, respectively. Immigrants so classified were considered to have Class A defects and therefore immediately excludable. Class B medical problems, which indicated that the patient might become a charity case, included nervous affections and senility. In these cases, the immigrant still might be granted entry depending on the inspector's opinion based on his observation and the medical certificates. In all cases, physical and mental, the concern was that the immigrant or their progeny would become dependent as a public charge.[30]

An immigrant could undergo a mental or intelligence exam more than once if doctors were undecided. Newly arrived, many prospective entries were sick

Figure 5. An immigrant pulled off the line for separate questioning. The Public Health doctors apparently thought this immigrant looked suspicious in some way, because of either suspected mental problems or low intelligence. Courtesy of William Williams Papers, Manuscript and Archives Division, The New York Public Library, Astor, Lenox and Tilden Foundations.

from the voyage, tired, fearful, excited, and thereby not showing their normal psychological state. Public Health Service doctors recognized that aliens often arrived in a poor mental state from the trip, and for this reason they often allowed suspect arrivals to stay over for a day or so, giving them time to rest, eat, bathe, and be retested. The doctors decided how long to hold the immigrant before further testing, which could be two or three testing sessions. In the mental room, doctors would first ask easy questions such as simple addition or how to do basic household chores. The ideal room conditions meant keeping the room at a comfortable temperature, with at most three individuals there. Testers were to "have a pleasant and kindly manner" and the room a soothing presence.[31] However, these stipulations were not always met.

Even a seemingly simple question asked of a woman, such as "How many children do you have?" could be misunderstood as to indicate that the woman was mentally deficient. For example, did the doctor mean how many children alive and dead did she have, how many children did she have with her at the moment, or how many did she have including those still in Europe and already in America? As another example, an inspector asked this question of an Irish immigrant: "If I gave you two dogs and my friend here gave you one, how many would you have?" The immigrant answered "four." When asked the same question in regard to apples, he answered correctly. Asked the question about dogs again, the immigrant once again said "four." The inspector inquired how could that be, and the immigrant answered, "Why sure, I've got a dog at home myself," and that made four. On the question of whether gold or bread would be tossed over the side if in a small boat at sea which had too much weight, if the arrival answered bread, that would be considered an illogical answer.[32]

Other tactics to determine mental state included asking immigrants to count forward and backward, memory tests, retelling a story read twice to them, identifying animals, and arranging or placing forms into their proper spot on what was called an imbecile form board. These last tests required, for example, fitting "rectangular blocks with square or rounded ends and circular blocks into larger recesses in a board" or putting "five rectangular blocks into a rectangular frame" within a certain time limit. Immigrants were also required to touch the same objects as the examiner in what was called a Visual Comparison Test.

Failure here could bring a second exam the next day with different doctors. An interpreter was present to explain the exercise. In the case of a 14-year-old Russian Jewish boy tested on two consecutive days, he could not count backward, did not know the months of the year, passed the form test but only on retrying, and did not know any colors but red. Doctors also asked him about the number of legs on a horse and a dog, and he had to do various other diagnostic puzzle board tests. The doctors rated him an imbecile and sent him along to the immigrant inspectors to make the final decision. An 8-year-old Greek boy at the first testing did not do well, as he cried through the exam. He was held over for another examination and at first was so scared that he could not speak. He then failed to answer questions correctly. The interpreter explained "in a most kindly way to the boy, that he was holding up the entire family; that tomorrow he must do better." The next day he passed. Emotions in a new and frightening setting played a role in the testing.[33]

Figure 6. An immigrant taking an intelligence test using blocks to fit into particular spaces. Others look on, waiting for their turn. The immigrant being tested must have felt pressured with other immigrants standing right behind her. Courtesy of National Park Service and website at www.ellisisland.org.

For the doctors it was significant not only whether the immigrant passed the tests but also how quickly the test was completed, how the immigrant looked while doing the test, the muscle coordination involved, and the ability to concentrate on the task. A number of tests had to be done poorly before exclusion, and the doctors had to see other signs of mental deficiency. An immigrant failing one test while doing well on others and having a good manner would not usually be deported.

However, examining doctors often had the option of determining the various categories of imbecile, moron, or idiot at their whim; some doctors with a eugenic bent thought that mainly southern and eastern Europeans fit into these categories. The concept of mental deficiency took on significant importance in a period in which eugenics suggested that immigrants having such problems degraded the nation's biological health. Dr. Howard A. Knox, a medical officer at Ellis Island from 1912 to 1916, was involved in developing and putting in place the intelligence tests used at the island. But it was testing with a particular bias. Knox said in 1913, "With special reference to the examination of immigrants it may be said that the detection of morons or higher defectives is of vastly more importance than the detection of the insane." The insane, he continued, would eventually be discovered and either institutionalized or deported "so that in either event they cannot propagate and affect the race adversely. On the other hand, the moron will not be recognized and will immediately start a line of defectives whose progeny . . . will go on forever . . . costing the country millions of dollars in court fees and incarceration expenses." In a 1915 article Knox provided the two reasons that mental examinations were done at all. The first was, as noted, to exclude immigrants who would "become a burden to the State or who may produce offspring that will require care in prisons, asylums, or other institutions." But he went on to say that "the same measuring scale could . . . be used in industrial enterprises to determine the intelligence, and hence the probable efficiency of illiterate or poorly educated aliens seeking employment."[34] Knox felt that some immigrants were throwbacks to an earlier human. He thought that a Finnish immigrant might be the missing link between ape and human which scientists theorized existed. He also said that he would eventually find an immigrant with a tail, indicating an earlier human species.[35] Excluding those who might become a public charge, those who would not become good workers in an industrializing America as a result of what was assumed to be hereditary factors, or those who were of an inferior "race" and intelligence was the primary motivation behind the extensive testing.

Dr. Alfred C. Reed, another Ellis Island doctor, wrote in 1913 how immigrants had changed from earlier times: "Previous to 1883, western and northern Europe sent a stalwart stock . . . They sought new homes and were settlers. Scandinavians, Danes, Dutch, Germans, French, Swiss and the English islanders, they were the best of Europe's blood. They were industrious, patriotic and far-sighted. They were productive and constructive workers." As for the southern and eastern Europeans, he continued, they "are less inclined to transplant their homes and affections." They tend to earn and go home, "they contribute little of lasting value but the work of their hands . . . In contrast to their predecessors, the immigrants since 1883 tend to form a floating population. They do not amalgamate. They are here to no small degree for what they can get." He concluded that the "changing and deteriorating character" of this type of immigration "makes restriction justifiable and necessary."[36]

Notions of "racial inferiority" influenced Ellis Island doctors, much like many other Americans. Madison Grant's writings, particularly his *The Passing of the Great Race* (1916), argued for the superiority of the Nordic, western, and northern Europeans in contrast to all others. The sense was that "unfit" immigrants were now entering the country and had to be curtailed. Immigration commissioner William Williams in 1911 described the new immigrants as "backward races . . . without the capacity to assimilate with our people as did the early immigrants," and in 1912 he wrote an article titled "Invasion of the Unfit" in which he warned against the entry of what he called "these lumps of poisonous leaven."[37] As a result, Williams employed a harsh observance of the immigration laws in regard to ability to earn a living. Not all doctors or immigration officials thought this way, but clearly those who did were more inclined to reject what they considered to be inferior people. Generally, negative stereotypes of eastern and southern Europeans, especially Jews and Italians, were prevalent in America. An earlier typhus epidemic associated with Jewish immigrants and nativist newspaper stories focusing on Italian crime and violence reinforced unfair descriptions of disease and crime as characteristics of these people. The stories about a few would be applied to the general immigrant population from those European areas.

Other doctors might be more sensitive to an arrival's cultural heritage and more willing to realize that the immigrants could make a contribution. Some, such as Dr. L. L. Williams, definitely felt that one test did not fit every immigrant and that immigrants should not be excluded on the basis of only one test. Even those biased against the immigrants, such as Knox, could acknowledge that the tests did not tell the whole story and that a deficiency in schooling was a contributing factor to low test scores. Knox felt that transient psychological problems could be mistaken for serious mental issues and cause the immigrant to be rated as having low intelligence or other problems. One interesting test asked an immigrant to interpret a picture of three elegantly dressed children burying a dead rabbit. The picture, labeled "Last Honors to Bunny," could be construed in numerous ways depending on culture and life background. In this picture, the boy was digging a hole, one of the girls had flowers in her hand, and the other girl looked on sadly. While most native-born Americans would understand the concept of burying a pet, European immigrants of peasant background would have trouble comprehending that a rabbit could be a pet, why the animal was being buried in a way that indicated a special event, and why flowers were needed.[38] The difficulty of analyzing how immigrants of different cultures responded to these tests made them less useful. Generally, given the newness and controversial nature of psychological and intelligence testing during this period, doctors tended to rely on their own experience, instincts, and observation, especially of the immigrant's physical appearance, to determine the mental state of the arrival. However, many intelligence tests were used or experimented with at Ellis Island, giving doctors or researchers much information to analyze for future determinations of mental issues. Doctors never found a single test satisfactory in determining mental ability. When new psychological tests were introduced, occasionally even doctors had trouble with the puzzles. At times, as in 1910, the newspapers or political leaders focused on the supposed poor quality of immigrants arriving at Ellis Island, and doctors felt pressured to find more cases of feeblemindedness or other mental problems. Experts in the field of mental testing were brought in on occasion to perfect the intelligence testing. Questions of cultural insensitivity or bias were constant concerns. Nonetheless, immigration inspectors deported more immigrants for feeblemindedness after reports about improper procedures that allowed inadequate immigrants into the country.[39]

Immigrants put into detention for further mental observation sometimes became so distraught that they committed suicide, indicating actual mental problems or desperation after the long journey. The mental exams resulted in many sad stories. La Guardia wrote, "I always suffered greatly when I was assigned to interpret for mental cases in the Ellis Island hospital. I felt then . . . that over fifty per cent of the deportations for alleged mental disease were unjustified. Many of those classified as mental cases were so classified because of ignorance on the part of the immigrants or the doctors and the inability of the doctors to understand the particular immigrant's norm, or standard." He mentions one case that particularly upset him:

> A young girl in her teens from the mountains of northern Italy turned up at Ellis Island. No one understood her particular dialect very well, and because of her hesitancy in replying to questions she did not understand, she was sent to the hospital for observation. I could imagine the effect on this girl, who had always been carefully sheltered and had never been permitted to be in the company of a man alone, when a doctor suddenly rapped her on the knees, looked into her eyes, turned her on her back and tickled her spine to ascertain her reflexes. The child rebelled—and how! It was the

cruelest case I ever witnessed on the Island. In two weeks time the child was a raving maniac, although she had been sound and normal when she arrived at Ellis Island.

In another case, doctors put a 15-year-old Swedish arrival in 1924 into detention for eye problems and then for crying and nervousness. The doctors determined that this behavior indicated mental deficiency and deported her after an appeal failed. Her mother returned to Sweden with her, while the rest of the family went to Massachusetts. This family was never together again.[40]

Disease Classifications and Cases

As with mental defects, Class A disease classifications also consisted of physical diseases that were immediately excludable but could be treated at the hospital if someone (individual, aid society, shipping company, or government) paid for the treatment and hospital stay. Sometimes this treatment could last months or over a year, but if the remedy secured a cure, the person would be admitted. This category would include diseases that were "loathsome or a dangerous contagious disease." Class B diseases were categorized as those making the immigrant "likely to become a public charge." Medical physical problems of the Class A type included, for example, trachoma, tuberculosis, venereal diseases, ringworm of scalp, and leprosy. The number and type of diseases increased over the years. Class B authorized the inspectors to determine whether the immigrant might become a public charge. Exclusion could be ordered, but the inspectors made this decision. This category included, for example, cancer, eyesight, varicose veins, hernia, heart disease, anemia, and pellagra. For those who looked like they could not endure hard work, even poor physique, although not an official category, could be used to deny entry. Pregnancy was put in either Class B or Class C, a category of minor concern, depending on the medical official's judgment and ultimately that of the immigration inspectors.

Often, the immigrants' occupation, intended settlement area, and how the disease would affect their work and ability to earn a living determined admission. How strict the immigration commissioner at the station wanted to interpret the laws was also important. Commissioner Williams, for example, was intent on harshly interpreting the law in regard to ability to earn a living. Would a defect such as a missing finger or eye be a detriment to finding a job?

This last stipulation became the most important in considering the immigrant's acceptance or rejection. Most immigrants pulled off the line for medical reasons were in Class B, and therefore in a group whose outcome was unclear.

In one case, Dante Pavoggi, whom officials detained at age 13 in 1911 as a result of swollen neck glands, was eventually accepted since the officials found out that he would be living on a farm and, therefore, would probably recover in a healthier environment than a city and meanwhile would not infect many people. However, Israel Bosak, arriving in 1906 from Russia after losing his tailor shop in a pogrom, was rejected owing to poor physique. Eugenic criteria dominated in this case, with the concern that he would pose a threat to America in relation to his progeny, who might perpetuate "the physical degeneracy of their parents." In a similar situation, Wolf Konig arrived before the Board of Special Inquiry in 1912 at age 17. The doctors rejected him for "lack of physical and sexual development for age claimed which affects ability to earn a living." Konig's uncle, already in Chicago and owner of a stationary store, promised to make sure that Konig would not go on charity. The Hebrew Immigrant Aid Society (HIAS) fervently but unsuccessfully defended the immigrant by claiming that "we believe that he can improve himself and his development with the assistance of his relatives who are prepared to help him to get better nourishment and exercise . . . Being a young boy, and not accustomed to travel, it is quite natural that this first long journey should cause him to become fatigued and to look poorly developed when examined." Even after some congressmen intervened, he was deported back to Poland. Clearly not all poor physique cases ended in deportation. Officials rejected Bartolomeo Stallone, coming to America in 1911 at age 16, initially as a result of physique issues that would make it difficult to find a job. On appeal, he was allowed in on bond, and he went to St. Louis, where he worked with his brother as a barber. After two years, officials lifted the bond and considered him fit to live in the United States.[41]

Appeals in all situations could be made to the secretary of commerce and labor, and, in some cases, even the commissioner of immigration at the island was overruled. Commissioner Williams rejected Chaie Kaganowitz, a Russian Jewish widow, in 1912, along with her nine children. He was concerned that they would become a public charge given the mother's eyesight problems and the children's poor physiques. Even though the children's ages went from 3 to 20 and the older two were carpenters, Williams considered the children to be weak looking, although all of them had passed the medical exam. The secretary of commerce and labor Charles Nagel did not have the same opinion since the older children had skills that would be usable to earn a living in America. After being held in detention for a month, the family was finally let in.[42] Many decisions, especially in regard to "likely to become a public charge" or unable to earn a living as a result of poor physique, were subjective; positive or negative judgments were based on who was doing the judging.

Technically, poor physique became an issue because it was associated with nonpulmonary tuberculosis. But more was involved; in practice, it involved the question of who (nationality, race, and class) should be allowed to enter. Poor physique was eventually defined in 1907 as meaning an "alien . . . is afflicted with a body not only but illy adapted to the work necessary to earn his bread, but also poorly able to withstand the onslaught of disease." This person was therefore "undersized, poorly developed, with feeble heart action, arteries below the standard size; that he is physically degenerate, and as such not only unlikely to become a desirable citizen, but also very likely to transmit his undesirable qualities to his offspring." Also referred to as "poor physical development, poor muscular development, and lack of physical development," the condition, although never a legislated reason for exclusion, did lead to detentions and exclusions.[43] A 1907 immigration law did allow exclusion if a condition would have a negative effect on receiving a livable wage. Among the Public Health Service doctors any definition was controversial and not fully accepted, but it aided the nativist/eugenicist cause regarding the entry of certain groups into the country. For Ellis Island, the definition homed in on eastern and southern Europeans; at Angel Island, for Asian immigrants, and especially Chinese, exclusion became the objective.

The *New York Times* ran an article in 1909 noting complaints against Williams that the charges of poor physique and inability to make a living wage targeted Jewish immigrants. Eugenicists eagerly portrayed Jews in this way, and a major controversy erupted over the exclusion of Jewish men on these grounds. Williams was at the center of the dispute because of his well-publicized prejudices against southern and eastern Europeans and his interpretation of the regulations and laws. More immigrants faced exclusion under his reign or were sent back within the three-year probation period, and this angered the ethnic press as well as the steamship companies that had to carry the rejected individuals back at the companies' expense. Although most immigrants still were accepted for entry, the increase in exclusions did occur under Williams's years as commissioner.[44]

Figure 7. Jewish immigrants in 1907 receiving a special physical examination in a separate room after doctors told them to leave the line. Doctors could have suspected a heart or lung ailment or a variety of other health problems. Naturally, this raised the tension level for immigrants and family members. Courtesy of Library of Congress, LC-USZ62-22339.

Moral Concerns

Moral concerns played a role in admission or exclusion as well; although never clearly defined, they ranged from adultery to murder. An integral aspect of the Progressive movement consisted of protecting American morals, which meant safeguarding middle-class notions of sexual mores, especially as they related to women. Inspectors sometimes designed immigrant questioning

Figure 8. Immigrants in 1902 in a detention pen on the roof of the main building. Detention meant that something was wrong and could lead to days or months in unsanitary and crowded quarters, as well as deportation. Courtesy of Library of Congress, LC-USZ62-116223.

to find sexually immoral women (but usually not men). For example, whether an unmarried woman was pregnant and whether a single woman was sexually active on the voyage over became matters of concern. Swedish immigrant Elin Maria Hjerpe arrived pregnant but single in 1909, although her husband-to-be traveled with her. She was initially excluded, but on appeal and with her fiancé's willingness to marry her right on Ellis Island, she secured admittance. Rulings in appeal could be based on the immigrant's homeland's moral norms. Marriage at Ellis Island resolved situations of arriving women suspected of immoral behavior. One immigrant male adulterer already living in the United States and married, but still within his three-year probationary period, was excluded from reentering the United States from Canada but eventually allowed in, as the secretary of commerce and labor

Oscar Straus said, for the sake of the well-being of his family in Massachusetts. But confusion generally held sway in all such rulings. It was not clear whether individual cases of sexual misconduct should lead to exclusion if the immigrant, as the solicitor of the Commerce and Labor Department said in 1911, was "clearly not of an essentially immoral character."[45] That statement seemed to say that earlier cases such as with Hjerpe should not have been initially excludable.

The admission of prostitutes significantly concerned immigration officials and reflected contemporary moral standards. The 1907 Immigration Act excluded women and girls who tried to enter or entered the United States for prostitution or other immoral reasons, as well as the pimps who ran the trade. The Progressive Era's anti-vice campaign and the crusade against white slavery (forcing women and girls into prostitution) led to this legislation. One young Croatian woman was arrested for prostitution within her three-year probationary period. She denied the charge, confessing instead to having sex with many men but never for financial compensation. Officials ruled that any woman who "for hire or without hire offers her body to indiscriminate intercourse with men" could be considered a prostitute.[46] The Croatian woman was deported. In 1909, immigration officials detained 573 immigrants as prostitutes at Ellis Island and sent 273 back to their homeland.

For Asian immigrants, especially the Chinese, an effort had begun in 1875 with the Page Act to exclude prostitutes, and this attitude continued in the Angel Island period. Chinese women faced constant suspicion of prostitution and thereby lowering U.S. moral standards if allowed to enter. Chinese men's efforts to bring over their wives were often met with hostility from immigration officials. Proving marriage required official documentation or a white person's acknowledgement that the marriage was real. In San Francisco and later at Angel Island, as at Ellis Island, indications of higher class marked by status and riches brought an easier entry into the country and less suspicion of immoral behavior. The binding of women's feet, a Chinese custom for upper-class women, also became an indication of a higher class and therefore led to easier entry.

Women brought back to Ellis Island on charges of prostitution were put into detention until their cases could be resolved. The women's treatment often depended on the immigration commissioner's own view of the women's lives. Commissioner Howe (1914–1919) was generally sympathetic to their plight, which he felt arose out of poverty or abuse. He even reversed some deportation orders. As he said, "I have, I admit, thought of the poor, ignorant, immoral women detained at the Island as human beings entitled to every help to a fair start in the world."[47] And he concluded that of the many accused prostitutes he had allowed to enter the country and afterward tried to rehabilitate, only a few had fallen back to immoral lives. Other immigration commissioners were not as generous toward suspected prostitutes.

Completion of Processing and Appeals

Those who went through the medical inspection successfully moved immediately to the final step with the immigration inspector, who, accompanied by an interpreter and sometimes a registry clerk, had the power, unlike the doctors, to exclude, accept, or return the person to the medical examiners. Basing his decision on all the regulations in force and armed with the immigrant's background, medical, and other information, the immigrant inspector had the means to make a judgment. Immigrants with Class A medical issues found quick exclusion. Those taken off the line and sent for further examination and then cleared went on to the immigration inspector. All others went to the Boards of Special Inquiry. Immigrants accepted up to this point moved into the Registry Room area, still according to their ship manifest group, and waited for the inspector to call them. As the immigration inspector called each individual by manifest number, he asked questions to make sure the immigrant was the one listed on the ship manifest and who could answer queries about his or her background and intentions, had the appropriate amount of money required for entry, and (after 1917) could pass a literacy test. Most of the inspector's questions came from the immigrant's information on the original ship manifest at the departure port. Immigrants could be detained or excluded at this point for medical, public charge, or other reasons. If they refused to answer questions, answered incorrectly, or challenged the inspector's right to ask questions, they could be excluded or detained for further study. Inspectors received a circular describing what they should look for in regard to mental issues. "Evasive answers to questions, uncertainty as to dates and places . . . incoherence, obvious misstatements, and undue reticence are a few of the suspicious characteristics to which attention has been called in the circular." According to a 1913 description, at this point lying was particularly evident: "Most of the immigrants have been coached as to what answers to give. Here an old woman who says she has three sons in

America, when she has but one. The more she talks, the worse she entangles herself. Here is a Russian Jewish girl who has run away to escape persecution. She claims a relative in New York at an address found not to exist; she is straightway in trouble."[48]

Mistakes could be made as well. Louis Adamic had this experience because the person listed to meet him at the island was incorrectly noted as his uncle rather than as a friend:

> The inspector fairly pounced on me, speaking the dreadful botch of Slavic languages. What did I mean by lying to him? He said a great many other things which I did not understand. I did comprehend, however, his threat to return me to the Old Country . . . My heart pounded . . . I was weak in the knees and just managed to walk out of the room . . . I had been shouted at, denounced as a liar by an official of the United States on my second day in the country, before a roomful of people.[49]

While most detained immigrants went into separate examination rooms, they could also be sent to special dormitories, or possibly to areas where a delousing and disinfection process would take place, or to the hospital. Immigrants temporarily detained had a cross placed next to their names on the ship manifest and were given a white card; those to be held for special inquiry had "S.I." placed next to their name and received a yellow card on which officials wrote the reason for detention. The head of the Boarding Division and the law clerk obtained reports of card-holding immigrants who did not appear for further examination. Detainees could not enter the country without an explanation regarding their detention. Immigrants with contagious but curable diseases such as mumps went to the hospital. Some immigrant women and children, detained because no relative or friend had come for them or because they had no money, either found help from one of the aid societies or were deported. First-class arrivals were, as always, treated differently. If a first-class person was detained, the superintendent of the Registry Division had to be notified in a special communication. These cases had high priority.

Detainees had the right to go before the Boards of Special Inquiry (created with the 1891 Immigration Act) to make a case for acceptance into the United States. These administrative boards, numbering up to eight held simultaneously in the busiest periods, made the final decision regarding acceptance or exclusion. It was a tense moment for an immigrant who had to appear before one of them. The boards saw constant use as 70,829 hearings

Figure 9. Immigrants in 1903 dealing with their last requirement, interrogation by the inspectors, who would have access to the immigrant's medical and other information and would also ask questions using the ship manifest as their source. Any discrepancies between the manifest and the immigrant's answers or problems with any other information could lead to detention or rejection even at this stage of the process. Courtesy of William Williams Papers, Manuscript and Archives Division, The New York Public Library, Astor, Lenox and Tilden Foundations.

took place just in 1910. At first four and then, after 1903, three immigration service officials officiated at these hearings and served as judges to determine the fate of the immigrant, although the boards were not considered to be courts. If two board members voted against entry, the immigrant would be deported. Testimony from relatives and friends, as well as an interpreter to make sure that everyone understood the proceedings, would be allowed as part of a defense. A social service agency's staff member could also be present to aid the immigrant. The board members questioned the immigrant first and then the witnesses (who had been waiting in a separate room) on basic facts about the immigrant's background and on the issues that led to detention.

Questions could range from whether they paid for their own travel to naming their relatives in the United States. Health concerns became an issue if that was the main factor of the immigrant's detention. In many cases, the board accepted the immigrant even if the Public Health doctors had certified various health problems. The special inquiry board heard all pertinent materials both pro or con regarding the immigrant, and since these proceedings were not considered judicial but administrative hearings, information not admissible in a court could be used here. Detainees suspected of becoming charity cases if admitted became the largest group brought before the board. The criteria used to determine whether someone would become a public charge consisted of occupation, physical ability to work at that occupation, the need for that type of worker in the United States, and the number of those in this country and in the immigrant's country of origin who would depend on the person's earnings. Most importantly, the immigrant had to become self-supporting. In situations of wives and children traveling on to husbands and fathers, the inspector needed some evidence that the family would be supported.

In one case, a single mother arriving with four children had to take an oath on a Bible that none of them "would ever become a burden on this country."[50] Numerous immigrants appeared before the board, although most were allowed to enter the United States. A dissenting board member or the immigrant could appeal through various immigration officials and eventually to a board of review, part of the Labor Department in Washington, D.C., but this type of appeal was not the usual practice. Those found excludable at the hearings would be summarily deported if no appeal occurred. However, as with many procedures at the station, ways could be found around negative decisions. An immigrant whom the board excluded would often turn to the immigrant aid or ethnic societies. The society would contact a congressman who may have had one of the immigrant's relatives among his constituents. Even if the congressman had previously supported exclusion in such cases, he would favor entry in a situation in which a constituent had ties and would use congressional influence to secure admittance. Newspapers would often take up the cause as well, appealing to the public's sympathies regarding the splitting of a family if the immigrant was not given entry and reprehending the stiff-necked, overly harsh attitude of the inquiry boards. The public and officials could experience strong emotions for an individual caught in the immigration machinery. Secretary of Commerce and Labor Nagel, who had intervened in the Kaganowitz case, admitted, "I am frank to say that my sympathy is all for the human side. I have sometimes felt that I forgot my own country and the law of my country in my desire to help out and to relieve the hardships of individual cases." Furthermore, he understood the impact his office could have. As he commented, "I can send back anybody. It is an awful power, but I try to use it to the best of my ability."[51] Nonetheless, he won the favor of neither pro- nor anti-immigration forces.

Cases could be complex and agonizing to decide and often tested the board members' judgment. Philip Cowen, an Ellis Island inspector, wrote of interesting cases he had observed. In one situation, a Polish mother and child were brought before the board because her husband, living in Buffalo, had not communicated with her since prior to sailing. Immigration officials asked the Polish Society to make contact with the husband and found that he had been in an accident that damaged his speaking and hearing ability. He also was illiterate. In that situation, the board felt that his family would become a public charge. However, during the course of the hearing, a workmen's compensation law, passed earlier, took effect. Under this new law, as the Polish Society found, the husband was eligible to receive compensation that would allow him to have enough funds to permit time for recovery and to support his family. His wife and child were therefore accepted into America.[52]

Angel Island Processing

The process at Angel Island worked differently. Chinese, Japanese, other Asian, and European arrivals were split into distinct groups for examination. The Angel Island medical and other exams varied from those at Ellis Island. First-class passengers, as at Ellis Island, received a medical exam on the ship. Steerage and second-class passengers (as of 1912 for the latter) went to Angel Island. But the Europeans received a perfunctory checkup, looking for trachoma and briefly checking their bodies, a less intense inspection than at Ellis Island and less intrusive than for the Asians. These Europeans were primarily Russians in opposition to and threatened by the Communist takeover and Polish, Lithuanian, or Russian Jews fleeing from religious persecution or, later, escaping from the Nazis. Some initially were denied entry based on the same criteria used at Ellis Island: medical, likely to become a public charge, contract labor, or other restrictions. But even among those, most received permission to be admitted after an appeal. Angel Island's rejection rate for Europeans was lower than that at Ellis Island. The Angel Island inspectors, consumed as they were with excluding Asians, did not indicate hostility to the Europeans and rather showed them favoritism. They did not usually indicate anti-Semitic attitudes. As with all immigrants, officials asked background questions. However, inspectors tried to help the Russians of all religions when they pointedly asked if the immigrants were fleeing religious persecution. A "yes" would aid in their acceptance, and immigrants were pushed to say "yes." Ellis Island inspectors did not offer this aid. Essentially at Angel Island officials trusted Europeans in their answers and gave them every opportunity to be admitted.

A good example comes from the use of the literacy test. Zlota Schneider, a Jewish immigrant, came to Angel Island in 1917. She could not read in any language and came penniless. At her hearing for the literacy test, the inspector tried to help her pass this requirement on religious persecution grounds. The inspector asked, "Were you disturbed at all in your home country on account of your race, being a Hebrew, or on account of your religion?" "Are you seeking admission to the United States to avoid any religious persecution in your native country?" Schneider did not take the obvious hint and answered "no" to both questions and was set to be deported. HIAS appealed the case and found that as the wife of an immigrant already residing in the United States she did not have to pass the test, and her husband could also support her. She had claimed initially that she was unmarried because the Russian government had refused to authorize her marriage, and she had to leave Russia as a single woman. The secretary of labor received an appeal in this case, and she was admitted. Crucial in this situation were not only HIAS but also the inspectors who desired entry for her. This favoritism was not apparent with Asians.[53]

Asians, especially men, received more rigorous assessment. Men had to remove all their clothes and be evaluated from head to toe. Both genders had to produce a stool sample to be tested for various parasitic diseases, especially hookworm. This examination forced the immigrant to remain on the island overnight or longer. Unlike the Ellis Island medical inspection line, Angel Island medical personnel relied more on a lab workup since doctors did not think they could know the medical problems with Asians simply by watching them stand and walk. The medical exam, and particularly the effort to find parasitic diseases, represented an attempt to root out Asians, and particularly the Chinese, who as a group were considered unsuitable immigrants even if American industry needed them. Deemed to be more inclined to sicknesses that threatened the nation than European immigrants, the Chinese experienced more intense examinations with the intention of prohibiting their entry. The Public Health Service, by overemphasizing the danger of hookworm and other parasitic diseases in Asians, used this exam as a way to exclude these immigrants, even though the infections could be cured. After much protest and infighting between the Immigration and Public Health Services, immigrants with parasitic conditions were regarded as not excludable based on this medical problem if they secured treatment. Prior to that change, most initially excluded Asians became so certified as a result of parasitic-related problems. By 1926 and 1927, almost 75 percent of Asians were certified in this way. The Public Health Service, most interested in excluding Asians as a group that did not belong in America, did not consider their medical problems in relation to ability to do industrial work. This more intense examination for Asians meant that not all nationalities and races experienced the same procedures. The Chinese immigrants' attitude toward the doctors can be surmised by the following poem excerpt from one immigrant:

> I cannot bear to describe the harsh treatment
> by the doctors.
> Being stabbed for blood samples and
> examined for hookworms was even more
> pitiful.

This immigrant continued by noting their "harsh treatment" and fear of the doctors. Mr. Lee, who came to Angel Island in 1930 at 20 years of age, said, "When we first came, we went to the administration building for the physical examination. The doctor told us to take off everything. Really though, it was humiliating. The Chinese never expose themselves like that. They checked you and checked you. We never got used to that kind of thing—and in front of whites." Chinese who were returning to China for a visit also were given harsh treatment. They were separated into an enclosure and questioned fully and recorded as to their personal information. Those Chinese returning to the United States were matched against a list in order to determine if they were actually U.S. residents.[54]

Immigrants who passed the medical exam went on to the feared interrogation. Angel Island inspectors were very severe in their questioning since they had to follow the Chinese Exclusion Act. Inspectors also had to deal with the issue of paper sons in determining eligibility. Even if an immigrant had papers, the inspector still had to be convinced that the documents were legitimate. Basically, the inspectors judged the Chinese as guilty of having fraudulent papers unless they could provide other credible evidence for admission. Immigration officials carefully scrutinized luggage contents for indications that the immigrant was lying. Questioning could go on for hours or even days. Inspectors cross-examined married couples separately to see if they had the same responses to questions. In one excessive interrogation, an individual had to answer about 900 questions. Immigrants also spoke of the inspectors' intensity, rudeness, and, at times, threatening demeanor.

Large files were developed for every Chinese immigrant; as San Francisco immigration commissioner Samuel Backus stated in 1911, "the proper disposition of one Chinese case may require stenographic work equal to that required in the handling of several hundred aliens of other races." Perhaps an exaggeration, but clearly the Chinese faced a different processing experience. As noted above, Chinese women had an even more intensive interrogation, including questions about any sexually immoral behavior. The process had detrimental effects on the Chinese, already filled with anxiety about the screening process. According to a Chinese woman who commented on the treatment of another, "One woman who was in her fifties was questioned all day and then later deported, which scared all of us. She told us they asked about her life in China: the chickens and the neighbors, and the direction the house faced. How would I know all that? I was scared."[55]

In another case in 1917, Lau Dai Moy arrived at Angel Island and said she was the wife of a much older Chinese man who claimed to be an American citizen. Both were suspected of lying, and each faced extensive questioning. The inspectors looked for mismatched answers. Questions included the following: "Q: What presents or ornaments has your husband given you? Q: When did your husband give you the hair ornament? Q: Did he buy that hair ornament in his home village? Q: Did you really wear the gay head-dress and the head[ed] veil at your wedding? Q: Just when did you wear the head dress? Q: How long did you wear the head dress? Q: Did you wear it while you served tea? Q: Who were the guests that you poured tea for?"[56] The inspectors designed this type of questioning to find small mismatches between answers, thereby giving cause for exclusion. Immigrants found further questions about their home and other marriage details difficult to answer even if married. In this situation, both were put into detention for six weeks for further study.

Furthermore, officials asked Chinese asserting citizenship pointed questions concerning the city—be it San Francisco, New York, or elsewhere—that they said was their home area. Europeans did not have to take this test. For Chinese who said they resided in San Francisco in 1906 during the earthquake of that year, exacting answers were required of what activity they had engaged in and where they were at that time. Had an English language speaking test been given to Europeans claiming citizenship, even after years in the United States, many would have failed. The testing had a racial motivation that whites did not face, even those from southern and eastern Europe. Chinese who were citizens but failed an arbitrary test could be deported.

San Francisco commissioner of immigration John D. Nagle in a 1927 statement illustrates how the inspectors behaved when he admitted "that his officers were 'reluctant to accept defeat' and would reexamine applicants and witnesses on 'every conceivable point' until they had found a discrepancy." One immigrant, Mr. Leung, in 1936, commented that "my deepest impression of Angel Island now was the rudeness of the white interrogators. They kept saying, 'Come on, answer, answer.' They kept rushing me to answer until I couldn't remember the answers anymore." Chinese stereotypes could be found in Americana newspapers, among customs and immigration officials, and in the general American public. The Chinese were considered duplicitous, intelligent, crafty, immoral, and made up of criminals. Whites were warned to be careful in dealing with them, and one newspaper said of immigration officials that it "required 'all the ingenuity that a white man always requires in dealing with the Chinese.'" The commissioner-general of immigration commented in 1900 that this group had "totally different standards of morality." Southern and eastern European negative images and stereotypes existed as well, but not on the same level as with Asians, especially Chinese. As a result, Chinese immigrants, expecting to meet a hostile environment at Angel Island, studied carefully from books, had coaching teachers who reviewed the questions that might be asked, or brought along coins and other materials that had the answers on them. For example, notes could be hidden in peanut shells that had been split and then
together. Immigration inspectors tried harder to break the immi
the immigrants made greater efforts to prepare for the inter
immigrant noted that with the amount of detail that had
you based your departure date on when you would
memorization.[57]

The coaching material was extensive and detailed. Providing this information became a business with writers who specialized in coaching books. The paper son's entire background was laid out as to village, relatives, jobs, and other pertinent details. These writers understood what questions would be asked and asserted in one such publication that "you will be asked whether there are any bricks, chickens, dogs, or photographs in your house." In another publication, the writer provided numerous questions and answers for the immigrant. For example, this book included the following:

> Q. Has your house an ancestral loft, shrine shelf, and tablets? What [are they] made of?
>
> A. Yes, We have an ancestral loft, a shrine shelf and five ancestral tablets. The shrine has two sections, the upper section contains the tablet for the goddess of mercy; the lower section holds the tablet for the entire ancestry of the family in the center, those for great grandparents on the left and those for the grandparents on the right. The shrine shelf has carved figures painted in gold.[58]

Coaching books also contained village maps indicating who lived in each house and where each house stood. They provided descriptions of every person in every house.

James Louie, arriving at Angel Island in 1932 at age 11, commented, "I was questioned three different times. The examiners asked all kinds of questions about your village, your grandmother, and how many windows do you have in your house? They also always questioned the paper father (my uncle) and my paper brother (my cousin) as witnesses. Whatever was not written down beforehand, whatever was not prearranged, then the answers you gave wouldn't be the same among all three of you. We didn't match up." As a result, to avoid deportation, immigrants at times offered bribes to immigration officials, which inspectors sometimes accepted. Inspectors particularly looked for discrepancies in detail among relatives and husbands and wives. Discrepancies in testimony from the records or from what other family members said could lead to deportation. Albert Kai Wong, coming to Angel Island in 1934 at age 12, remembered being questioned a number of times. He noted that "people around me were worried all the time. They had come in fictitiously and they had to learn what answers were correct."[59] Questions ranged from important family dates to minute details of village life: Who were your neighbors? How many rooms did the house have? What material was used to build your house? The detail was so explicit that at times even legitimate sons could be rejected. As a precaution, interpreters for the various immigrant and family member interviews were never the same individual. As one inspector noted, fear of collusion between the immigrant family and interpreter prompted this tactic.

One apparent contradiction between family members' testimony, but actually was not, reveals the confusion that could be evident. As the interpreter who served in 1928 related regarding the inspector's questions,

> A mother and two kids came in at the same time, and a question by the inspector was: "Is there a dog in the house?" If you live in a house, you know whether there's a dog or not, especially if the dog is your pet. So the mother said, "Yes, we have a dog." And another son, "Yes, we have a dog." And the third son, "No, no dog." So they called in the mother again, and the son, and they both said, "Yes, yes, we had a dog." And the other son was called in again. "Did you say that you have a dog in the house?" "Oh, we had a dog, but we ate that dog before we left! No dog! Well, this was true. By the time he left the house, there was no dog. So, otherwise, it would be a very serious discrepancy if you lived in the same household and two said there's a dog and the other one said no.[60]

Angel Island also had its Boards of Special Inquiry and an appeal process, as at Ellis Island and other processing points. The Chinese actively fought the exclusion laws, with numerous law firms hired to appeal, lobby, and help the applicants complete all their paperwork. In one situation, a 12-year-old's questioning took 87 pages in order to chronicle the interrogation and testimony, but the decision called for deportation. An appeal to the federal court reversed the judgment. Chinese women also made effective use of the appeal process. Even after all the inquiries and fears of immigration officials about allowing immoral women to enter, just a single Chinese woman was denied entry to the United States on the charge of prostitution in the 1910–1940 period. More than 76 percent of Chinese immigrants appealed their exclusion in the 1910–1924 period, with 39 percent securing entry after their appeal. If this tactic did not work, some tried to enter again and obtained admis[illegible] In all, just 7 percent of Chinese arrivals at Angel Island did not suc[illegible] securing admission.[61]

The Chinese Exclusion Act led to Ellis Island restrictions o[illegible] as elsewhere, but the Angel Island experience was mor[illegible]

Island Chinese Division came into existence around 1920 to deal with Chinese immigrants who might have arrived illegally, particularly through being smuggled into the country from Canada or arriving as sailors. Earlier, anyone the Chinese Exclusion Act barred came under the Special Inquiry Division's supervision. Efforts to block Chinese immigration included a New York Chinese Office under the Bureau of Immigration which investigated cases of illegal immigration. Contact was also maintained with the Angel Island office to determine if they had information on the immigrant or his family. The Chinese faced even harsher negative stereotypes than European immigrants, and their presence was an unwelcome one in America. Edward Corsi, immigration commissioner at Ellis Island from 1931 to 1934, depicted the Chinese as a threat to American workers, and "their religion and ancient beliefs, their contempt for western civilization and their resistance to Caucasian assimilation have always been considered as a menace to American institutions."[62]

The number of Chinese entering the United States, even with the exclusion laws, led to concerns among many Americans who wanted to limit this population. Much like Ellis Island immigration, constant cries were heard about too many immigrants, and especially the wrong type being accepted. But as with the Europeans at Ellis Island, strong pro-immigration voices fought for immigrant rights. Some Americans pointedly expressed unease at how the Chinese were "welcomed" into the United States and what effect America's negative attitudes might have. Max Kohler, assistant U.S. district attorney in New York, said in 1901 that "instead of welcoming them like other aliens, we have denied American citizenship to the Chinese, discriminated against them, and established this monstrous deportation and exclusion system against them, which is based upon the assumption that they have none of the 'rights of man.' How could we possibly expect them to be assimilated as other people are?"[63]

Other Requirements for Entry

Regulations required that all immigrant arrivals have some money with them so as not to be considered likely to become a public charge. Although the amount changed over the years, $25 was the highest sum requested at Ellis Island, occurring when William Williams returned as commissioner of immigration in 1909. At first this requirement caused serious problems, as $25 was a large sum of money at that time. Detainment increased and delayed entry for numerous immigrants. Williams's actions represented his attempt to exclude those who might become public charges, as well as to suggest an amount that would enable immigrants to support themselves until they found a job. But this demand caused controversy, and he backed off and said that the amount was not a reason to exclude. The issue involved whether a property test for admission existed. While Williams had wanted such a requirement, official policy had no $25 proviso, although he continued to suggest such a policy. In 1910, he said that "this office repeats that immigrants will not be allowed to land without funds adequate for their support."[64] Therefore, the $25 requirement remained in immigrants' minds, and confusion continued with regard to what funds were obligatory to enter.

Alexander Rudnev, a Russian Jewish immigrant detained on Ellis Island with many others in 1909 owing to this "requirement," wrote a letter to the *Jewish Daily Forward*, America's main Yiddish newspaper, signed by 100 other Russian Jews, to inform the Jewish community that they were imprisoned on Ellis Island. "Many of the families sold everything they owned to scrape together enough for passage to America. They haven't a cent but they figured that, with the help of their children, sisters, brothers, and friends, they could find means of livelihood in America." Fearing a return to Russia, they appealed for help. "If we had known before, we would have provided for it somehow back at home."[65] Rudnev secured admission, and Secretary of Commerce and Labor Nagel negated any amount stipulated. Inspectors sometimes disregarded the entire issue. Aaron Chaifetz, arriving from Russia in 1913, worried during the whole inspection process because he had only $22 with him. When he got to the final inspector, he said, "'I haven't got enough money.' So the guy says, 'Go ahead!' They wouldn't even count them." Charles Anderson, arriving from Sweden, did not have the money either. However, when the inspector asked whether he had the money, he said yes and was admitted.[66]

Acceptance and Entry

After approval at Ellis Island, those immigrants who had to wait for a friend or relative to come for them were classified as "New York Detained," those who could leave immediately and go on the ferries to New York as "New York Outsides," and those to be taken to rail stations for travel to other cities as "Railroad." Immigration officials would accompany these individuals to the rail stations and see that they went on the appropriate train. If the relative or friend did not arrive by the end of the day for those labeled "New York Detained," immigrants were provided with places to sleep. Having a sponsor arrive late to pick up an immigrant could be another factor in the emotional roller coaster evident at Ellis Island, even for those who had passed through easily. Marie Jastrow, arriving as a child with her mother in 1907, waited for their father, who already resided in America. "And my father was late. The minutes passed, one by one. A million catastrophic possibilities assaulted our imagination. 'Where is Papa? Was there an accident? Has he forgotten that we were coming? Is he coming at all?' . . . My mother's eyes filled, and I panicked." They did not want an immigration inspector to notice their distress, but one did. "An immigration inspector came upon the scene and as was the case with immigrants, they froze . . . at the very sight of a uniform—any uniform."[67] Even at this point, an immigrant could be sent for further study if an inspector thought someone was acting oddly.

Immigration inspectors considered the elderly a special case, and they were almost always detained until a relative or friend came to meet them. As Frank Martocci relates, "At the Island, these poor unfortunates would wander about, bewilderment and incomprehension in their eyes, not knowing where they were, or why they were being kept." They looked for those who knew their language. Martocci, as an Italian interpreter, was always being approached with anxiety-laced questions: "Have you seen my son? Have you seen my daughter? Do you know him, my Giuseppe? When is he coming for me?"[68]

Before immigrants' arrival, the social service agencies tried to contact their relatives and tell them the date of arrival so they could plan to take a ferry to Ellis Island to meet their family. For the immigrants, a staircase with three railed sections was available at this point, dramatically referred to as "the Stairs of Separation." One led to the ferry boats going to New York. Another went to the railroad ticket office, from which immigrants could go on barges to the appropriate railroad station. And the third went to the detention rooms, where those waiting for friends or relations stayed.[69]

Those waiting in the railroad room would receive a box of food for their travel from the aid societies. Jewish immigrants would be provided with a cheese sandwich that was kosher, other immigrants with a ham sandwich. A can of sardines, bread, an orange, and some salami or bologna were also often in the box. It was not unusual at Ellis Island for attention to be paid to cultural aspects of food if possible and also to religious service. Immigrants could also buy more food. Those wishing to buy food did so under a sign that read, in five languages, "Provisions cheaper here than on the railroads."

Immigrants also experienced new foods at this time. One immigrant confronting a slice of bologna "smelled it carefully from different sides, licked it, finally tasted it, and then broke into a flood of smiles."[70] Others were bewildered by what Americans considered commonplace items. Rita Seitzer, a 19-year-old immigrant from Lithuania in 1921, remembered seeing staff people at Ellis Island in the Great Hall area standing in the balcony and chewing. "I was thinking to myself, 'What is that? Is that a sickness here? They all keep chewing.' Until I talked to my family later, they explained to me that this was chewing gum," which was unknown to her.[71] Immigrants' relatives or friends who came to meet and vouch for the new arrivals and those scheduled to speak before the Boards of Special Inquiry on behalf of an immigrant relative or friend also had a waiting room for their use. If a relative came with incorrect papers, officials detained the immigrant, as happened to Celia Adler in 1914. She was fed and sent to sleep in a hammock. "I remained sitting on the hammock all night. I didn't sleep a wink." The next day her sister came with the proper papers, and Celia was released.[72]

Emotionally laden scenes of immigrants and relatives finally meeting after years of separation or perhaps never having met before filled these final moments on the island with confusion, great happiness, and pathos. Old photos held tightly in hands frequently became the only identification other than names. "Are you my uncle?" and "Are you my brother?" were not uncommon questions asked at the last Ellis Island stop. Judith Cohen Weiss came to America after World War I to be with her father and reunite the family. "So when my father came, they told him he would have to wait. I did not even know him. When he embraced me, I got very frightened because he had a little beard and mustache—I had never seen this. So I was frightened and started to cry. My sister came over to me and said, 'What are you crying about? It's Papa.'" Sonya Kevar, arriving from Russia in 1911 at age 13, had a similar experience after not seeing her father for five years. "I couldn't recognize him. I kept looking at him and looking at him . . . He was dressed differently, too. He was dressed like an American." Rose S. speaks of her and her mother meeting their relatives and their reactions:

> I wanted to go home, and so did she. Oh, how we wanted to go home! She came to two sons, and she didn't know them. They were away for eleven

> years. At Ellis Island, these two young men came up and stood right next to us. We don't know who they are, they don't know who we are. That's a terrible thing. They spoke English, they were married, they have children, and you can't visualize those things when you think, "Oh, I haven't seen them for eleven years, but when I see them I'll recognize them." It's not always the case.[73]

Where detained immigrants reunited with friends and relatives was appropriately named the "Kissing Post." At this point, family and friends, either immediately or after finally acknowledging each other, embraced and kissed, signaling arrival in America and the ingathering of families.

The whole process at Ellis Island seemed to some like a factory, moving immigrants along on a virtual conveyor belt. As Stephen Graham, who traveled in steerage in 1913, wrote about his experiences, "It was interesting to observe at the very threshold of the United States the mechanical obsession of the American people. This ranging and guiding and hurrying and sifting was like nothing so much as the screening of coal in a great breaker tower. It is not good to be like a hurrying, bumping, wandering piece of coal being mechanically guided to the sacks of its type and size, but such is the lot of the immigrant at Ellis Island."[74] And yet, fitting into the industrial system was exactly what the immigrant was supposed to do.

3 How Newcomers Dealt with Delays and Coped with Detainment or Rejection

Hot, filthy, and congested detention areas, rats running around, and sometimes inedible food describe some of the conditions at Ellis Island. Illegal aliens sneaking into the country also took place at the island, bringing a historical connection with present-day illegal/undocumented immigrant issues.

The system of gaining entry into the United States, then as now, was not foolproof. Illegal immigrants managed to get into the country through various means, and those deported were not always justifiably excluded. Sometimes, the hysteria brought on by war, the Communist Revolution in Russia, strikes, bombings, and inflammatory speeches and newspaper reports led to violations of civil liberties and the misuse of Ellis Island. The most publicized case of deportation occurred in 1919 when government officials rounded up 249 individuals suspected of anarchist and radical activities during the Red Scare and sent them to Russia. Among those deported were Emma Goldman (who had arrived in America in 1885) and Alexander Berkman (who had arrived in 1888). The SS *Buford*, better known in the press as the "Red Ark," carried the group back. This deportation clearly indicated that once in the country, immigrants could still be deported for violating U.S. laws. What was the process for delaying, detaining, or deporting immigrants? How were detainees and those deported generally handled?

Some illegal immigrants were stowaways on ships or had made arrangements with captains or crews to be allowed on board for a bribe. Immigrants could secure false papers, hide criminal documentation, and forge medical records. On one occasion, three immigrants left a ship with crew members to get past the guards on the dock. Claiming to be part of the crew and vouched for by actual crew members, they entered America.[1] Furthermore, officials sometimes disregarded regulations, especially for first- and second-class passengers.

Ellis Island detainees were a mixed lot and included many who would later be admitted after further scrutiny. Jacob Riis, an investigative journalist who wrote so poignantly about the inhabitants of New York's slums in *How the Other Half Lives*, described in a 1903 article those detained at Ellis Island: "Here are the old, the stricken, waiting for friends able to keep them; the pitiful little colony of women without the shield of a man's name in their hour of greatest need; the young and pretty and thoughtless, for whom one sends up a silent prayer of thanksgiving at the thought of the mob at that other gate, yonder in Battery Park, beyond which Uncle Sam's strong hand reached not to guide or guard. And the hopelessly bewildered are there, often enough exasperated at the restraint, which they cannot understand."[2]

Orphans represented one specific group detained. A *New York Times* article in 1906 depicts the plight of 30 Jewish children orphaned by the Russian pogroms. Coming to the U.S. without parents and underage meant that they would be immediately detained. The National Committee for the Relief of Sufferers by Russian Massacres appealed for these children to be accepted. Sarah Perlmann, their guardian, had brought them to America, and the United Hebrew Charities cared for them. With many letters arriving which expressed a desire to adopt the children, there was no question of finding homes for them. As a result, they secured admittance.[3]

Detainees, Schools, and Education

Ellis Island immigrants could be detained overnight or longer, with sleeping facilities usually grossly overcrowded. Besides detaining those with a particular health or other issue, immigration inspectors also detained family members or friends traveling with them. Women and children had matrons assigned to aid them during this difficult time. Officials provided food, lodging, and religious services for all immigrants and offered school classes for children. Nothing formal in education was developed until 1915, when official schools, under commissioner of immigration Frederic C. Howe's reforms, became available. The Congregational Church in concert with the immigrant aid societies and the Red Cross ran these schools, which children of varied nationalities in detention voluntarily attended. Children were detained for different reasons: a parent in the hospital, a parent who had not yet come to pick them up, or even a child waiting for the family to be deported. Or a child could be in the hospital while getting some schooling. As such, schooling for a child could be abruptly cut short. As Bertha Boody, who studied the schools in 1922, commented, "A child who started work in the morning might be on a train or a tug boat by afternoon." School officials went to the detention areas each day and asked the children whether they wanted to go to school. Those who did got into a line and proceeded to the school area, which had a rooftop playground. School classes implemented a variety of ways to keep the children busy, as well as in some cases to learn. Available were arts and crafts, singing, receiving instruction in the English language, and information about their new country. Angela Maria Pirrone (Weinkam) arrived at Ellis Island from Palermo, Italy, at age 12 in 1924. With her mother hospitalized, Angela stayed in detention for 31 days until her mother recovered. She went to school three days a week and started to learn English. She remembers the playground, taking walks on the island with the aides, and every day at 3:30 p.m. getting milk and graham crackers. Other than school, she sat in the hallways and talked to other detainees. Besides this basic learning experience, the children received psychological tests, mostly for the purpose of seeing which tests would be most appropriate and useful for a larger population. Finding which nonverbal tests could be applied at Ellis Island especially interested the examiners. Most children who opted for school were in the 10–14 age group. Older children usually showed little interest.[4]

Americanization instruction was also a function of various societies such as the Daughters of the American Revolution. In what represented an effort to instruct the immigrants about American culture, these societies focused on history and civics, among other topics. They attempted to provide the immigrants with American historical heroes and give lessons in what it meant to be a good citizen. Efforts to Americanize continued after entry primarily through the public schools, settlement houses, and foreign language press. Learning English signified an important aspect of Americanization. For those in detention at holiday times such as July 4th, Christmas, and Passover, the staff celebrated the various holidays with the detainees.

For hospitalized children, officials made special endeavors, as a 1921 report noted, "to maintain morale, to hasten recoveries, and incidentally to impart instruction as to the ideals of American life . . . These children are taught to read and write English, to be courteous and respectful, to be patriotic, to sing national songs and salute the flag, and to observe the ordinary rules of hygiene."[5] The instruction took place in the hospital wards with children separated according to their disease. In all matters, many Ellis Island personnel tried to help detained immigrants begin their adjustment to America.

As of the 1910s, activities offered adults consisted of concerts, films, athletic competitions, and courses in knitting, maintaining personal cleanliness, and raising a child, much more than Angel Island provided. About 20 years after opening, Angel Island's detainees' own organization, the Angel Island Liberty Association, bought a record player, Chinese opera recordings, books, and other material to help pass the time. They also offered entertainment occasionally and a school as of 1932. Ellis Island had libraries with books and other reading material in a number of languages, contributed by a variety of organizations and individuals.

Detention Conditions

However, detention at Ellis Island was a stressful time for all. Men went to one area and women and children to another, splitting families. Those detained in inadequate conditions included everyone held for any reason, except for those sent on to the hospital. Cleanliness was always an issue in regard to the kitchen, detention areas, and dining room, with immigrants contributing at times by leaving debris on floors. The overcrowding of various areas prevented thorough cleaning.

Detained individuals could easily contract diseases while in custody. And as Frank Martocci remarked in 1907, "It was almost impossible to provide strict sanitation . . . With so many people packed together under such conditions, it was naturally impossible for them to keep clean, for the clean ones were pressed against aliens infected with vermin, and it was not long before all were contaminated." The detention areas also remained closed to visitors. In 1909, Commissioner William Williams commented on the detention facilities: "When there are from 800 to 1000 persons packed into these quarters . . . the conditions are indescribably bad. The toilet facilities too, are inadequate and the ventilating system is incapable of carrying off the foul air."[6]

Dining also presented problems. Leah Shain, an Ellis Island immigrant in 1921, describes the dining hall: "I remember coming into a long, dark room with very long tables of bare wood. It had wooden benches not chairs. We heard lots of languages from all kinds of family groups. You had to share these tables . . . But it really didn't matter because we were all in the same boat—everybody was miserable."[7]

With up to 2,000 Ellis Island detainees per day in 1907, feeding the immigrants became a consistent challenge. Martocci relates that "one employee brought out a big pail filled with prunes, and another some huge loaves of sliced rye bread. A helper would take a dipper full of prunes and slop it down on a big slice of bread, saying: 'Here! Now go and eat!'" It was not always as bad in less crowded years, but nonetheless, as Martocci continued, "the poor wretches had to obey, though they didn't know where to go. They moved along, their harassed faces full of fear, with their [detention] cards held dumbly in their hands." The food eventually improved after corruption was rooted out, but problems remained. Helen Barth of the Hebrew Immigrant Aid Society noted how unclean the kitchens were and the many rats that inhabited the island. Also, the food manager was making money by providing the cheapest possible food for the immigrants. Ellis Island staff, visitors, and anyone who had some money could go to a separate dining room with better food and better accommodations, including items such as table clothes, napkins, and silver service, although it did cost more to eat there.[8]

Food service and the concessionaires who had food contracts caused major problems at Ellis Island over the years. How is such a diverse population fed in a satisfactory way? Commissioner Henry Curran commented in his memoir about the problem of "building a menu to suit the palates of sixty different national tastes. It was American food. If I added spaghetti, the detained Italians sent me an engrossed testimonial and everybody else objected. If I put pierogi and Mazovian noodles on the table, the Poles were happy and the rest were disconsolate. Irish stew was no good for the English, and English marmalade was gunpowder to the Irish . . . There was no pleasing anybody. I tried everything and then went back to United States fodder for all."[9] The meals served in 1924 to the hospital patients were as follows: breakfast always consisted of some variety of oatmeal, eggs, bread, and coffee; lunch could include soup, corned beef, pot roast, spare ribs, hamburger, veal, fish or beef stew along with potatoes, and a variety of vegetables, as well as dessert; dinner was frankfurters, macaroni and cheese, baked beans, or cold meat along with a range on different days of prunes, coleslaw, stewed tomatoes, pickles, rice, and desserts such as cookies, gingerbread, apple sauce, sliced peaches, and, with every dinner meal, tea. For most immigrants generally, with the exception of those in the hospital, the menu in July 1921 consisted of boiled rice with milk, stewed prunes, and coffee for breakfast; lentil soup, lamb, vegetables, pudding, and coffee for lunch; and bologna, mixed salad, apple sauce, and tea or coffee for supper. While the range of food was of sufficient nutrition, the quality and service were not always the best at either island station. One Chinese detainee at Angel Island offered the following description in 1922: "The melon was chopped in pieces thrown together like pig slop. The pork was in big, big chucks. Everything was thrown into a big bowl that resembled a washtub and left there for you to eat or not as you wished. They just steamed the food until it was like a soupy stew . . . After looking at it, you'd lose your appetite!"[10] On one occasion in 1925, the unhappiness with the food caused a food riot.

Sleeping quarters were crowded as well, with detainees sleeping in three-layer bunks with little distance between the three sections and other bunks. These sleeping quarters, even in the biggest dormitory for men, were often pushed to the limit. Williams in 1911 noted that "when all of the beds are occupied, as frequently they are, the congestion in this room is very great, and since it has only an easterly exposure the temperature on summer nights may be 100." A Russian Jewish detainee's letter to the editor of the *Jewish Daily Forward* in 1909 stated that "it is impossible to describe all that is taking place here [at Ellis Island], but we want to convey at least a little of it. We are packed into a room where there is space for two hundred people, but they have crammed in about a thousand. They don't let us out into the yard for a little fresh air. We lie about on the floor in the spittle and filth. We're wearing the same shirts for three or four weeks, because we don't have our baggage with us." Conditions continued to be deficient into the 1920s. Elizabeth Dobbin of the National Catholic Welfare Conference wrote in the organization's bulletin in 1921 that "accommodations at Ellis Island are inadequate when immigration is at high tide. In one day twenty-four hundred are packed in the detention room. The number of available beds will accommodate about eighteen hundred persons . . . yet it is a common occurrence to have more than two thousand persons detained over a period of a week or longer."[11] Immigration commissioner Frederick Wallis (1920–1921) remarked in 1921 that the dormitories had little fresh air; the windows were kept closed even though up to 400 people slept there when he observed the room. And the toilet facilities were inadequate since no toilet paper was provided. Also, towels and soap were not offered, although Wallis corrected both. However, in keeping with class distinctions, detained first- and second-class passengers were given separate sleeping quarters in rooms not overcrowded. A single bed was even provided for first-class detainees. Fresh sheets, pillows, pillowcases, and a mattress made the sleeping facilities much more pleasant for the higher-class immigrants.

Commissioner Williams noted that individuals waiting for entry into Ellis Island Boards of Special Inquiry rooms in 1908 to serve as witnesses for the detainees had "to wait for periods ranging from an hour to five and six hours. It has been estimated that at times 300 persons were endeavoring to get into this room and the stairway leading thereto being packed to suffocation. It contains no toilet facilities." In 1920, the newly appointed immigration commissioner Wallis reported on conditions for special inquiry detainees waiting for their cases to be heard. When he went to the special inquiry area, Wallis "found a guard keeping watch at the S.I. [special inquiry] door. When I asked him why he did not keep the door open to let some air in to the immigrants, he said that they ask too many questions. I told him he should be thrown out in the Bay . . . When I opened the door, the hot, foul, sultry air almost pushed me backward. There were several hundred immigrants in the room, and seats for not more than fifty. Men, women and children were standing all day or sitting on the dirty floor." Upstairs in another special inquiry room, "the stench being worse than downstairs . . . I found only one toilet room open. And even that one was stopped, the filth washing out on the floor where little children were playing." Also filthy was the recreation room, which held up to 1,500 immigrants. Wallis commented that "when you walked on the tiled floor you would slip in the slime." The floor had not been cleaned in a number of months.[12] Wallis immediately fixed this problem.

During World War I, excluded immigrants could not be returned to their homelands and therefore stayed in detention for the war's duration. Commissioner Howe tried to improve conditions for these individuals who had nowhere else to go. He allowed them more freedom on the island to socialize with others. And he allowed some of the immigrants classified as feeble-minded to enter the United States on bond. Commissioner Henry Curran began his service in 1923 (1923–1926) and commented on the poor conditions of the island environment. As he wrote, "The surrounding waters were thickly tainted with sewage, the patch of green had given way to several acres of added earth and rubbish . . . It was a poor place to be 'detained,'" with buildings filled with rats and mice and beds occupied by bedbugs. In the large detention rooms, "which housed every night two thousand immigrants, there were no beds at all. There were bedbugs, but no beds." Instead, wire cages, each holding one person, and each having one blanket but no sheets or pillows, were provided. The cages, as Curran continues, offered almost no ventilation. "It was a contraption that would make a sardine sick. I have seen many jails, some pretty bad, but I never saw a jail as bad as the dormitories at Ellis Island, where nine out of ten of the immigrants had never committed any crime at all." Curran secured a congressional appropriation to provide beds with mattresses, pillows, blankets, and sheets. He later said that "I had never seen such concentrated human sorrow and suffering as I saw at Ellis Island."[13]

Detainees did often feel as if they were in prison. Visitors could come only on Tuesdays and Thursdays. Commissioner Corsi (1931–1934) eventually opened up the station to the press and to visitors, who could visit with no restricted days. He also allowed detainees to have greater access to phones, now available in detention areas. The commissioner, in his effort to make Ellis Island a more livable space, further permitted detainees more time to spend outdoors. During Corsi's early years at the station in the 1930s, with Herbert Hoover as president, he was able to acquire funds to repair the buildings. Later, under President Franklin Delano Roosevelt, the Public Works Administration and the Works Progress Administration stepped in to make further repairs and improvements, such as an expansion of recreational areas. The commissioner also secured more separation between deportees and arriving immigrants and between different classes of immigrants. His more flexible approach and ability to improve the buildings came during a time when the federal government, through New Deal programs, funded many projects to put people to work as a way to enhance employment. But unfortunately, these improvements in many ways came too late since immigration numbers were sharply declining in the 1930s, along with detentions, and the more accommodating policies and upgrading could have been more effectively used in earlier heavy immigration years.

Although sleeping quarter assignments centered on class, whether arrivals came in cabin or steerage, nationality did not result in divided space even if some immigrants thought themselves of a higher and more refined class. British immigrants constantly complained about being forced to share quarters with "undesirable" immigrants of "dirtier and inferior nationalities." As early as 1903, these immigrants in detention objected to using blankets whose previous owners were non-British detainees. Commissioner Howe commented that the British were most problematic. "When detained, an Englishman would rush to the telephone to complain to the British Embassy." When deported, "he sizzled in his wrath over the indignities he was subjected to." Unlike Angel Island, where racism against Asians and especially Chinese ensured the separation of nationalities, on Ellis Island officials refused British demands for separate areas and exceptional rights. The British issue became so important that British government officials took the matter up with the U.S. government. Roland McNeill, in the foreign office, said "that the facilities at Ellis Island were basically for people 'of a low standard of conduct' and a hardship for those of 'any refinement, especially women.' " British ambassador to the United States Sir Auckland Geddes conducted a special tour of the station in 1922 and issued a scathing report on conditions, in particular as they related to British citizens. Geddes above all noted the low level of behavior and hygiene among immigrants, but he singled out only one group, indicating his own biases. "I have to think that it might be feasible to divide the stream into its Jewish and non-Jewish parts." He also said in disgust that he "saw one nice, clean-looking Irish boy examined immediately after a very unpleasant-looking individual who I understood came from some Eastern European district . . . The doctor's rubber gloves were with hardly a second's interval in contact with his private parts after having been soiled, in the surgical sense at least, by contact with those of the unpleasant-looking individual." Although he said he originally thought that a separation of nationalities would be the answer, after his inspection, he felt it was not feasible.[14]

Not all experiences were negative, even for those in detention. An Armenian immigrant writing to the *New York Times* in 1924 said that he and his large family had been in detention for 72 days. He spoke of good treatment by various departments of the station, including the school, dormitory, and hospital. Although he said he went "through long, unnecessary trouble on account of the absurdities involved in the quota restrictions . . . to ignore the many splendid arrangements, the good discipline in general and to call it a 'hell' is certainly unfair." He further noted that the "food supply and service could not be better under the circumstances" and that the hospital and school worked well. Staff treatment of the immigrants was praised, as well as arrangements for entertainment and religious services.[15] Obviously, with so many immigrants over so many years, it was not unusual for various opinions of the island station to be expressed.

Detention at Angel Island

Detention at Angel Island involved fewer people since immigration did not reach the numbers realized at Ellis Island. The Chinese made up most of the detainees owing to the exclusion laws, and detentions were often longer as a result of U.S. racist attitudes toward this group and the process of appealing a negative decision. European immigrants could pass through Angel Island relatively fast, but the Chinese could be in detention for months or years. In fact, Chinese immigrants experienced the longest detentions of any group at any port. The Angel Island hospital was also different from Ellis Island's in that the Chinese, Japanese, and Europeans were each put into different sections of the building. Immigration officials racially segregated dining rooms. The percentage of arrivals detained was much higher at Angel Island than at Ellis Island. Once again, Europeans at Angel Island had an easier time than Chinese in regard to detention rates and amount of time detained. As a result of different treatment, the Chinese detainees felt most burdened with emotional distress. Isolated, guarded, in crowded rooms, and restricted to certain areas, the Chinese were most likely to consider themselves in a prison. Food issues showed further problems and bias. The meals were below standard for all on Angel Island but worse for Asians. The government stipulated that less money be spent on feeding the Asian immigrants than the Europeans or island workers. As a result, in 1909, food providers spent 14 cents for each Asian meal, 15 cents for European meals, and 25 cents for employees.[16]

As at Ellis Island, conditions remained poor. Sanitation was rudimentary. The dormitories were overcrowded. In 1911, just a year after opening, a Chinese visitor to the facility asked the immigration commissioner, "Is this a jail . . . and must all Chinese imprisoned here be treated like felons? This is not the least unlike a cattle pen!"[17] The Chinese Benevolent Association in San Francisco consistently complained about the unsanitary situation that resulted in immigrants becoming ill. In 1932, the Angel Island Liberty Association, a Chinese men's detainee group, was still asking the immigration officials to make soap and toilet paper available to those in detention.[18] An indication of the Chinese detainees' dismay is found in the many poems they scratched into the detention barrack's wooden walls. As Li Hai wrote,

> It's been a long time since I left my home village
> Who could know I'd end up imprisoned in a wooden building?
> I'm heartsick when I see my reflection, my handkerchief is soaked in tears
> I ask you, what crime did I commit to deserve this?[19]

Another poem reads,

> Imprisoned in the wooden building day after day,
> My freedom withheld; how can I bear to talk about it?
> I look to see who is happy but they only sit quietly.
> I am anxious and depressed and cannot fall asleep.
> The days are long and the bottle constantly empty; my sad mood, even so, is not dispelled.
> Nights are long and the pillow cold; who can pity my loneliness?
> After experiencing such loneliness and sorrow,
> Why not just return home and learn to plow the fields?[20]

Officials housed European detainees in better quarters separate from Asians and detained or deported fewer Europeans. Sometimes, detentions turned out to be related to economic conditions in the San Francisco area and whether the individual might become a public charge. For Jewish immigrants, as at Ellis Island, HIAS was extremely effective in securing their entry. Whites also had their own recreation area, reflective of the racism evident at the time. Gender and class separations were required as well. Inspectors allowed all women and all Europeans to engage in activities such as taking walks beyond the detention restricted section rather than being largely confined to a negligible space, although officials supervised walks for Chinese women. Immigration officials intended to isolate the Chinese, as well as other Asians, from the white detainees, but given the overcrowding on the island, segregation was not always possible. Chinese men did have recreation time in the yard and had access to Chinese newspapers, books, records, and chess, but they essentially found themselves imprisoned. Other detainees complained about a prison atmosphere as well, but the Chinese, with the largest number and the longest stay, experienced this more so. What help the Chinese detainees received came mainly from their own self-help organization or from the San Francisco Chinese community. One Chinese detainee described conditions in 1939: "I had nothing to do there. During the day, we stared at the scenery beyond the barbed wires . . . Besides listening to the birds outside the fence, we could listen to records and talk to old-timers in the barracks. Some, due to faulty responses during the interrogation and lengthy appeal procedures, had been there for years. They poured out their sorrow unceasingly. Their greatest misery stemmed from the fact that most of them had had to borrow money for their trip to America." Besides borrowing, like the Europeans at Ellis Island, the Chinese had sold their belongings and had nothing to return to, and "a few committed suicide in the detention barracks."[21]

About 85,000 Japanese arrived at Angel Island. Japan had assented to a Gentlemen's Agreement with the United States (1907–1908) which prevented Japanese and Korean laborers from coming to the United States, which reduced the immigrant numbers and controlled for unwanted immigrant workers. Therefore, those immigrants allowed to depart from Japan were able to obtain entry relatively quickly, but some faced long detentions similar to those for Ellis Island immigrants, owing to medical issues, appeals to prevent deportation, and suspicion of women immigrants as prostitutes. Most Japanese immigrants consisted of picture brides coming to America to unite with husbands secured through arranged marriages. For those detained, their experience, while not as appalling as the Chinese, could be equated to Ellis Island Europeans. Teiko Tomita, a Japanese woman arriving at Angel Island in 1921, said, "We didn't understand the language, and though they gave us three meals a day, their food did not agree with us. We all cried and cried because we didn't know when we'd be free and because we couldn't understand anything they said to us."[22] Although the YWCA and the Women's Home Missionary Society helped the Japanese learn English and American customs and worked to improve conditions, the women experienced a great deal of anxiety waiting for physical and other examinations. For Japanese picture brides, the questioning took place with their husbands alongside and contrasted with the intensity or number of questions for Chinese interrogations. Once the couple had proved they were husband and wife, officials required that they be remarried according to American standards.

Other Asians, Indians, Sikhs, and other "Hindus," as newspapers referred to them, had difficult times as well. South Asians lost their right to emigrate to the United States with the Immigration Act of 1917. Restrictionists, proclaiming the same arguments against South Asians as with the Chinese, asserted that they could not be absorbed into America and would take jobs away from American workers. Angel Island staff worked fanatically to exclude this group. Reasons for exclusion included hookworm, poor physique, liable to become a public charge, and contract labor, which were used to a much greater extent than at Ellis Island to prevent entry for these immigrants. Interrogators tried to trick immigrants into saying they had a job waiting, therefore making them excludable under contract law regulations, or that they had no job, therefore making them excludable as likely to become a public charge. The inspector's attitude and the government's view of a particular group remained important in determining admittance. America needed workers, but some remained more acceptable than others. Detention and rejection numbers stayed high.

As at Ellis Island, Angel Island had many organizations, including numerous ethnic and religious ones, working to make life better for the detainees with legal aid, help for those allowed to enter the United States, English classes, religious needs, social services, clothing, books, movies, and instruction about American traditions. On Angel Island, the Travelers' Aid Society provided help, the Chinese YMCA offered English instruction, and the Women's Home Missionary Society helped the Chinese with small tasks such as writing letters. Katherine Maurer, a missionary known as the Angel of Angel Island, represented the Women's Home Missionary Society of the Methodist Episcopal Church and served there from 1912 to 1940 fulfilling various roles in the religious and service categories such as implementing English classes, observing holiday celebrations following Christian traditions, and providing daily help to the detainees of all backgrounds. She was active in offering social services to the immigrants, writing letters, giving the arrivals clothing, following up with visits to their homes after leaving the island, helping them find jobs, and just serving as an advisor and good listener.

Ellis Island Immigrant Aid Organizations

Ellis Island immigrants who were detained, hospitalized, rejected, or had any other problems received assistance from various immigrant aid societies such as HIAS, the Italian Benevolent Institute, the Italian Welfare League, the Catholic Welfare Council, the Austrian Society, the Greek Society, the Salvation Army, or the Red Cross. This last organization, for example, provided

American-style clothes for women departing from the island before they saw their husbands, so that they would fit in better with their new country. The Salvation Army representative, along with other aid societies, could sit in on Board of Special Inquiry hearings, ask questions, and help the detained immigrants explain their situation.

HIAS was active on Ellis Island as of 1902 in advising Jewish and other immigrants in appeals if they were threatened with deportation (HIAS helped 3,726 individuals in just 1913), collecting evidence, locating family and friends, finding housing and jobs after admittance, aiding those who initially could not support themselves, defending those who did not arrive with the proper amount of funds, and assisting those charged for hospital stays. After entry, they helped with naturalization classes and secured housing and jobs. Immigrants needing aid could find it from those with blue hats bearing the initials for HIAS in Yiddish. HIAS also provided written instructions of advice for immigrants. For example, the organization's representatives assisted immigrants pulled aside for medical reasons and served as interpreters for them in the examination rooms. HIAS also worked overseas in trying to improve steerage conditions and providing information to Jews in Russia on eligibility requirements for entry into the United States.

Tessie Riegelman, who worked as a secretary for HIAS after World War I, said, "Immigrants used to come in crying and crying. My heart would break, and naturally you tried to do the best you could for them." Helen Barth relates that "we [HIAS] were making briefs out all the time . . . giving the government reasons why the family should stay and that the little child should be allowed to be treated at Ellis Island . . . The government let them slip through very often, very often, but we had to have it done legally." Immigrants encountering legal trouble after arriving or on their way to becoming a public charge became special concerns. Barth notes that "we saw these people through by helping them. We took care of their health, we gave them food, we gave them clothing, we gave them homes." HIAS was also instrumental in holding Jewish religious services on Ellis Island, securing kosher food by establishing a kosher kitchen on the island in 1911, and maintaining Jewish religious holidays. The National Council of Jewish Women and other aid societies saw that single girls and women going through and leaving Ellis Island received help in going to decent residences, securing food for the journey, and contacting relatives. The Society for the Protection of Italian Immigrants, created in 1906, and other Italian benefit societies would accompany Italian immigrants from Ellis Island to either New York City addresses or railroad stations.[23] These organizations had offices on the island and operated daily on behalf of the newcomers. Many more deportations, especially of eastern and southern Europeans, would have occurred without the presence of HIAS and other agencies.

HIAS also worked to limit Christian missionaries' efforts to proselytize among the Jews. Robert Watchorn, a Methodist and a commissioner of immigration at Ellis Island (1905–1909), also weighed in on this issue in 1908 when he informed the American Tract Society not to engage in missionary work among the Jews at Ellis Island. As he said, "A great many of our immigrants are Hebrews, who are on their way from persecution by one style of Christians, and when they have Christian tracts—printed in Hebrew—put into their hands, apparently with the approval of the United States Government, they wonder what is going to happen to them there." Officials stopped efforts to proselytize among the Jews until, as Watchorn later said, "the immigrants have rested from the effects of the hardships to which they have been subjected in countries in which their persecutors said they did their work for Christianity's sake." President Theodore Roosevelt supported this approach when he affirmed that "while the immigrants are in the Government's care missionaries, whether Protestant, Catholic, or Jewish, should work among their co-religionists so as to avoid any appearance of proselyting [*sic*]."[24] This approach appeared unusual in a period when religiously oriented settlement house workers and missionaries stayed active in immigrant neighborhoods on behalf of Protestant conversion. Once in their ethnic enclaves, especially in large cities, proselytizing went on unabated even after objections from Jewish and Catholic leaders.

For those deported, ships at the New York dock took them back to their homelands. Sometimes the home country would not allow the immigrant to return because of criminal or mental issues, and they remained stateless at Ellis Island. In some cases, mental patients were deported only to be institutionalized in Europe at U.S. expense. Many immigrants, including contract laborers, were sent home, often without funds as a result of the cost of coming to America.[25] At times, immigrants falsified their credentials and faced detention and deportation for that reason. One interesting occurrence involved an individual claiming to be a carpenter because he did not want to be labeled as possibly becoming a public charge. To determine if carpentry was indeed his occupation, the board of inquiry gave the immigrant the chance to prove his skills at the Ellis Island carpentry shop. Failing to prove that he could have been a carpenter, and since he also had little money, he was deported. Immigrants would go to great lengths to avoid deportation. Sarah Weadick of the National Catholic Welfare Conference wrote in 1922 of an Italian woman arriving with six children and ready to meet her brother. However, the board of inquiry determined that the brother would not be responsible for the children and therefore they might become public charges. With her and her children scheduled for deportation, the mother was forced to ask Weadick an unusual and clearly last-minute question: if she married her brother's friend, an American citizen, would she and her children be eligible for admission? Weadick inquired if she would be willing to marry this man, about whom she knew nothing. The Italian mother, not wanting to return to Italy and hoping to make a new start in America, said, "I grant you, Signorina, I did not come with that intention, but what would you do? They are about to deport me. One must make some sacrifice if one would enter your country."[26]

Since all immigrants were subject to a three-year probation during which they could still be deported if they became public charges, cases of this type existed as well. Commissioner Williams reported that in 1909 Chayge Rochel Schenker and her two children received permission to enter New York and travel to her husband. Subsequently, a third child arrived, and the husband abandoned the family. She was then forced to apply for charity in order to place her children in a public institution. The New York charity department notified the immigration bureau, which then reviewed the case, and the family was deported.[27] Immigrants who had legal, employment, or financial problems and were threatened with deportation would go to social service agencies such as the Salvation Army. In some cases, the Salvation Army was able to help those deported to reenter the United States by securing the proper documentation. But first the person had to go back to the old country. These organizations functioned beyond the time the immigrant left Ellis Island. Angela Carlozzi Rossi, executive secretary of the Italian Welfare League as of 1934, kept busy helping families whose breadwinner had been deported, assisting immigrants who needed to prove they came in legally, aiding them during the Depression in securing government relief, and offering advice.[28]

Friends and relatives testifying before the Board of Special Inquiry at times lied to secure a detained immigrant's acceptance. They would claim willingness to support the immigrant or state that they had a good job avail-

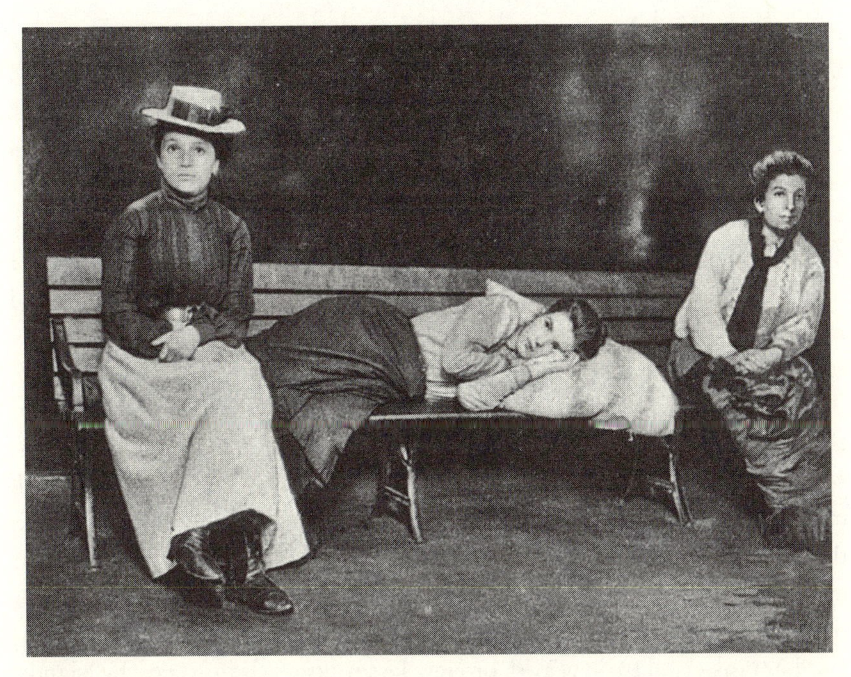

Figure 10. Three women rejected in 1902 and waiting for deportation on the same shipping line that brought them to Ellis Island. Many deportees had spent all their funds to get to America and now faced a dismal journey back, sometimes leaving family behind in the United States. Courtesy of Library of Congress, LC-USZ62-93250.

able for them. Immigrant aid societies or relatives offered a bond at times for immigrants considered a possible public charge. The bond guaranteed that the society or relative would ensure that the immigrant did not become a charity case. Immigration officials checked on occasion to ensure that the immigrant was not relying on charity. If all checked out, the immigrant could be admitted to permanent status; otherwise, deportation would occur. HIAS stepped in on a number of cases where the immigrant was set for deportation. As HIAS worker Sadie Guttman Kaplan, an earlier arrival at the island, said, "Our job was to intervene and take responsibility for them."[29]

Ellis Island Hospitals

The hospitals available on Ellis Island served basically for treating those arriving with curable diseases or with injuries or medical conditions that, as medical officer Dr. Victor Safford commented, "prevent a person from doing manual labor immediately." Those with mental disorders, even if considered cured, nonetheless faced rejection; deportation "would still be mandatory." Dr. Thomas Salmon said in 1905 that, according to the law, any individual considered insane within a five-year period, including their time at Ellis Island, would be deported. The emphasis was clearly on the ability to secure and hold a job in America. Dr. Safford noted that given the meager amount of money immigrants had upon arrival, it was "highly desirable that he should not be turned loose until his real asset, his physical strength, had been fully restored."[30]

Ellis Island's first hospital was inadequate to deal with major health problems such as cholera. Ships carrying cholera-infected passengers in 1892, referred to as "Death Ships," remained in the harbor, not allowed to dock until the disease had run its course. A doctor with authority at the port said that individuals who tried to disembark were to be shot. Epidemics terrified everyone, especially the 1,000 passengers and crew stuck on these ships for three weeks with contagious individuals. A few years later, patients could also be transferred to New York or New Jersey hospitals or to nearby islands, but concerns about bringing contagious immigrants into the city continued. After the 1897 fire that destroyed most of the facilities on the island, the federal government built new and larger hospitals. The first, opened in 1902, had space for 120 patients, eventually increasing to handle 275 patients. In 1907, the government constructed a hospital for mental diseases, the Psychopathic Pavilion, after two suicides occurred in 1906 among patients at the main hospital. One suicide involved a hostile and defiant man who had to be locked in a cell, but then used a wire from a light to hang himself; the other was a woman detained for mental examination who jumped out of a window. The last hospital to be built, the Contagious Disease Hospital in 1911 on the third island, had facilities to hold 450 patients and wards for specific diseases. Hospital staff and medical personnel who were single were able to stay on the island in facilities provided for them on the second and third islands.

One doctor, Milton Foster, remarked on the extensive hospital work being done: "It is by no means unusual to receive one hundred cases or more at the hospital in one day. The task of admitting, examining, treating, and housing this number of new patients in five or six hours, would tax the capacity of the largest hospitals in the country." And as Dr. Alfred Reed noted, the hospital saw a diversity of diseases from around the world, including "rare tropical diseases, unusual internal disorders, strange skin lesions" not seen in other U.S. hospitals.[31] In essence, Ellis Island treated the sick and infirm from every country. Nonetheless, the hospitals, as more buildings were constructed, provided more than adequate treatment with a modern diagnostic lab, four areas for operations, and top-rate facilities. If necessary, the doctors brought in specialists to help with the cases. A snapshot of hospital services in fiscal year 1906 records that the hospital admitted 7,464 patients, including 2,794 children. Of these, 59 adults and 268 children died. The average daily number of patients in the hospital was 242. Due to the heavy use of hospital facilities, the number of buildings and hospital types had to be increased over the years.[32]

Communicating with the patients was not always easily done. Given the number of languages the immigrants spoke and the fact that the hospital staff did not include interpreters, doctors and other hospital workers, unless they could speak another language, had to depend on the few foreign words they knew. In some cases, doctors called in interpreters from the immigration staff. The first procedure in the hospital for the arriving immigrant was to have them bathe. Immigrants at times resisted bathing since the new arrival feared that the staff was trying to confiscate their clothes, in which money often had been hidden. Josephine Friedman Lutomski, a ward nurse in the measles and chicken pox ward from 1922 to 1923, said that when the ill immigrants arrived at the hospital, "we would have to take them into this room and wash their hair and some of them had never seen a bathtub and were afraid to get in it and take their clothes off." Hospital staff sent clothes to be fumigated, and they subsequently were returned. After each bath, the tub had to be scrubbed thoroughly to avoid spreading contagious diseases.[33]

Immigrants often misinterpreted hospital staffs' actions. In 1920, a Polish woman strongly resisted an attempt to X-ray her for possible tuberculosis. The problem was that the woman thought the machine was a camera and did not want to undress for the procedure, fearing that this was an attempt to photograph her with no clothes and would provide the police with a nude picture of her. She insisted that "I am not a bad woman," indicating that only a wicked woman would agree to this course of action. On another occasion, a Bulgarian man refused to wear a bathrobe that a staff worker had given to him. Inexplicably, the immigrant patient was furious. Another patient clarified the situation and "laughingly explained that the Bulgarian would not wear the bathrobe because it was red. Red was a Turkish color," and the Turks were arch enemies of the Bulgarians. Of course, how would the attendant know about this ancestral loathing or, for that matter, any other Old World hatreds?[34] All patients and staff would see everything that occurred in the wards. The wards held up to 50 patients, and therefore little privacy existed.

Removing children from parents still remained a frightening concern for both patients and staff in 1922. Dr. M. Gertrude Slaughter reported that she often saw situations where the staff received abuse.

> It was in connection with the hospital that I saw one of the instances in which the attendants were the recipients of blows. Scarlet fever had developed in the child of an immigrant after the ship had passed quarantine. The parents were well and inspectors directed them to the first island, while the orderlies came with a stretcher to take the child to the contagious ward. Immediately the mother attacked the attendants, beating and scratching them, and then tried to throw herself into the bay because she thought her child was being taken from her forever. Another attendant then had to hold the mother gently but firmly until an interpreter could be found who spoke her language; he explained the situation thoroughly, and peace returned.[35]

Most patients did receive good treatment. As outlined in a memorandum covering procedures at the Contagious Disease Hospital, all tuberculosis patients had their rooms scrubbed daily, and all patients were to get as much fresh air as possible and exercise if they could tolerate it. Hospital workers conducted breathing exercises and mandated that patients spend a required time in bed. Patients also had to cover their mouth and nose with gauze when sneezing or coughing. Also patients, if able, could be taken to the recreation hall, where silent movies, billiard tables, a record player, and a piano were available. They would be allowed walks as well. Nurse Lutomski observed how much the patients enjoyed looking out the windows and seeing the Statue of Liberty. "They couldn't wait to see New York."[36] Social service workers were at the hospital every day to try to make the stay more comfortable, providing writing material and toys for children. The staff escorted visitors to the recreation rooms to spend time with their hospitalized relatives and friends. The ferry to the hospital islands, operated by the Department of Labor, ran hourly.

The hospital experience contained all the grief and joy of this Island of Hope and Island of Tears. Sad stories were constantly evident. One mother found that her baby had to be taken from her on the inspection line owing to the child's diphtheria, and she later learned that the baby had died. She had to go on the rest of her journey to meet her husband but without their child. In 1907, Mrs. Marie Gorda from Germany threw herself into the water after learning that her baby daughter had died from measles in the hospital. The father had come to America seven months earlier in order to raise enough money to bring them from Germany. He waited for his daughter to be released from the hospital, expecting to take his family home after a joyous reunion; instead, he found them in the Ellis Island morgue. In other cases, a mother and father could be detained for several months while their child was in the hospital, or a child would be detained for many days without seeing their parents or understanding the languages being spoken at the hospital, worried that they were being abandoned and would be sent back to the old country. In 1908, inspectors detained a mother, who came from Russia with her three young children, because she had trachoma. She was hospitalized for months at Ellis Island but could not be cured, and her husband, who had a job, could not afford to pay for her care beyond that time period. She was deported, thereby forcing her to abandon her husband and children in America. Anthony Merital, an Italian immigrant who arrived in 1910 with his mother and two siblings, found that both he and his sister needed ear operations. While they were recovering, his brother contracted scarlet fever and soon after died. "And at that time my mother was getting a little hysterical . . . she couldn't see her husband. They wouldn't let him in and the children are sick and now the baby died, so she had a rough time . . . And the bad part of all this was that we don't know where he was buried, what they did with him." Morris Moel, a Jewish immigrant from the Ukraine, in 1922 discovered that inspectors rejected his sister because she had trachoma, and she had to go, with a guardian, to Antwerp to get treatment. After a year and agreement from the Antwerp doctors that she was cured, she once again went to Ellis Island and again experienced rejection based on a diagnosis of trachoma. It wasn't until four years later that she could rejoin her family in America.[37]

Patients, a social welfare society, or even the shipping line could pay for the hospital stay. Sometimes, however, the federal government agreed to absorb the expenses. In one situation, inspectors admitted a 15-year-old German boy with trachoma to the hospital in 1908 after his father expressed willingness to pay. However, the father exhausted his funds after eight weeks, and he appealed to the Board of Special Inquiry for help. The father pleaded,

"Please help a German-American out of an embarrassing situation . . . I earn $18 a week, and I had saved $300 but now all my money is gone and I have to look out for my family here. I am willing to pay something, but cannot possibly raise so much. It would beggar me. I have always been a good citizen, have never been arrested, and have been a foreman ever since I am in this country. I think my son belongs to us, and he will make a good citizen." The board agreed to authorize payment for the son's hospitalization until he was cured three months later.[38]

While the hospital used the most modern techniques, it could not deal with some diseases that are curable today. And the possible cure then could often be painful and did not always work. For example, a trachoma "cure" involved a lengthy process of removing infected tissue under the eyelid with coarse substances in order to create scar tissue that protected the cornea. Yet, happy events occurred as well: children cured, babies born (which made them automatic American citizens), and families reunited and cleared for entry into the United States.

The hospitals were constantly busy. In 1911, doctors treated over 6,000 immigrants on the island. In 1912, Dr. Reed spoke to the reason the hospitals were so busy: "There was a constant stream of fresh infection pouring in."[39] Of course, some immigrants ended their journey on the island or nearby through death. In fiscal year 1908 alone, 267 deaths occurred on the island. All burials took place in New York City and not on Ellis Island. In some cases, immigrants trying to escape the hospital detention ordeal went into the water in a desperate effort to reach the mainland. Antone Belado did manage to reach the mainland after swimming from the island dressed in a hospital attendant's uniform, but he was arrested.[40] Even children harbored thoughts of escape. Flora Greenwald, who came from Poland in 1922, remarked, "I was very frightened, and I was very, very upset not to be with my mother. And I used to look out the window in the hospital . . . and I saw the lawns and I used to think to myself, 'How can I escape?' "[41]

4 How the Immigration Staff and Others Viewed Their Work

How did Ellis Island staff handle the workload? What did they think of the immigrants? Did corruption exist within this vast bureaucracy? Ellis Island had numerous workers, from medical officers to clerks to cooks. The staff dealt with detainees, maintained buildings and power plants, cooked and served, and ran the barges and ferry boats, among other tasks. In 1903, Ellis Island employed 350 workers split into 17 sections, including but not limited to medical, statistical, law, and janitorial. The island population also comprised representatives of companies that held government contracts to engage in businesses such as selling railroad tickets and various concessionaires providing and selling food. The shipping companies had landing agents at Ellis Island to oversee processing of those immigrants who had arrived on their companies' ships. In 1913, the medical division alone had 25 doctors split between the boarding, hospital, and line sections. Boarding medical staff headquartered at the Barge Office examined first- and second-class passengers on the ship after the initial quarantine inspection, hospital medical officers handled the patients at the island hospitals, and line doctors inspected the great mass of steerage travelers. Six medical officers dealt with mental problems. Work at the island was difficult and seemingly unending.

Commissioner Watchorn observed when he took his job in 1905 that "to receive, examine, and dispose of 821,169 aliens in one fiscal year is a work so stupendous that none but painstaking students of the immigration service could possibly have any intelligent conception of what arduous duties and unusual considerations it involves."[1] With fewer immigrants, Angel Island had a smaller workforce. Before the Angel Island facilities opened in 1910, the staff included about 10 each of inspectors and interpreters and about 30 of other professions (e.g., clerks, engineers, carpenters, cooks, guards, and others). However, by 1920, as immigration increased, the staff had grown to 137.[2]

Most Ellis Island staff did their jobs well, with efficiency and proper behavior. Employees had the use of dormitories, recreational areas, and dining rooms. Every worker had their own room. Kitchen personnel could eat as much as they wanted. Angel Island workers could live on the island if they desired, although the majority did not. Immigration officials provided cottages for those staff members, such as hospital employees, who had to be on the island for its daily functioning.

But how did these workers regard the immigrants and their own jobs? Dr. Gertrude Slaughter, one of the Ellis Island line physicians, said it best when she commented, "I approached my task with considerable misgiving, feeling that I had become part of the crushing mechanism. I soon learned, however, that although I was one of the watchdogs at the gate, I was expected to show as much kindness and consideration as possible."[3]

Dr. Bruce Anderson, who started at Ellis Island in 1919, noted that some doctors considered their assignment to the island as punishment for poor work elsewhere; an Ellis Island position was not a desirable one, except in the hospital. Work on the inspection line was considered physically exhausting. Yet, he felt that patients understood that the hospital doctors were trying to help them. He found both joy and sadness on the island. The joy came from seeing families reunited. "Unfortunately, times did occur when a family had to be separated because of deportation or death. Then (long pause), then you wished you were somewhere else." Dr. Robert Leslie, who spoke to the immigrants who were pulled off the line for possible mental factors or because of questions about their background, tried to calm them. He told them, "You are coming to the land of opportunity. You will have a chance to work, to live and to enjoy life. The police will not bother you. You won't have to carry with you your identification card." Speaking various languages, he was able to solicit more information. But the work, he said, "was emotionally difficult because I took with them their horrors and their emotional capacity." Leslie could only work three days a week because he found the work so arduous. On the question of whether line doctors felt badly when they had to certify someone as having a deportable disease, Dr. Grover Kempf, who was assigned to Ellis Island in 1912, remarked that the doctors had such short contact with the individual immigrant that an emotional involvement, at least for him, was precluded, except for hospital patients, especially children, who had more extensive dealings with the doctors.[4]

One immigrant, Jacob Auerbach, who arrived at Ellis Island from Poland in 1921, went on to become an immigration inspector in 1930. He said of his work,

> My job was to ask them questions, find out, check their papers, find out whether they are eligible to land, whom they are going to, and so on and so forth. Not very difficult . . . And I enjoyed it. It was beautiful. And the pay was very good. If I am not mistaken it was twenty-one hundred dollars a year. That was very good money in 1930 . . . It was good work, very interesting, meeting people, talking to them. And there was a very good camaraderie between a number of the inspectors; immigrant inspectors, were either themselves immigrants, maybe one or two or three, but most of them were sons of immigrants. Everybody had a warm feeling for the job and for this situation.

Auerbach said the inspectors treated the immigrant well, and it was the doctors that the new arrivals feared. Other workers, such as handymen, ward maids, garbage collectors, and clerks in the statistical division, had little direct contact with the immigrants, but their jobs were essential to the island's operation. Sadie Guttman Kaplan was another immigrant who went on to work at the island. She arrived from Russia in 1905 at age 12, and by the 1920s she was working at Ellis Island for the Hebrew Immigrant Aid Society. When asked how she felt, as an immigrant herself, dealing with other immigrants, she replied, "I felt very good. I knew what they were going through. I felt it . . . I was very considerate, tried to be more considerate, and have sympathy, tell them not to worry. We tried to do the best we can for them."[5]

Yet not all Ellis Island employees felt so benevolent toward the immigrants. American journalist Broughton Brandenburg, who gathered information on the immigration process, reports cruel treatment by those moving the immigrants to the barges. Pushing the arrivals onto the barge, one worker, when asked what he was doing, responded, "Oh, I'm driving these animals back." He continued, "You've got to be rough with this bunch. I get so sick handling these dirty bums coming over here to this country."[6]

At Angel Island, the staff was influenced by orders to make it difficult for the Chinese especially, but other Asians as well, to enter the United States, and some inspectors fervently worked to do so. Even the San Francisco commissioner of immigration, Samuel Backus, railed against Asian immigration in 1915, which he considered a danger to the country, and Chinese immigrants commented on the guards' harsh treatment of them. However, other guards never agreed with the exclusion laws. John Birge Sawyer, an inspector at Angel Island from 1916 to 1918, although sympathetic to the Chinese immigrants, had to follow the law. His attitude is revealed when he describes positively another inspector and his feelings: "[Inspector Charles Mehan] maintained a very sympathetic attitude toward every subordinate and every Chinese coming before the office. It was evident to me that he worked with higher motives than one generally finds among civil service officers. I have heard him tell of instances of injustice to Chinese and their patient submission to acts of injustice and indignities and then add that the Chinese needed a friend in the office he held and this made him contented in his work." Furthermore, Sawyer later spoke of the injustice of the laws, saying that they "had been an irritation and an insult to the Chinese for 61 years." He concluded that "one can hardly blame the Chinese who sought by wiles and crooked schemes to defeat our exclusion laws . . . Those laws stood in the way of their natural and commendable ambition to gain a better way of life." His thoughts about Ellis Island are also pertinent. When offered a position at Ellis Island in 1925 as a Chinese inspector, Sawyer said that he "found the atmosphere of the Island rather depressing and am sure I should never wish to serve there. The officers are unrefined and not well educated and their work is not of a sort to stir enthusiasm."[7]

Corruption, discrimination, and improper treatment did exist among those who came into contact with immigrants at both islands. At Ellis Island, workers hired as a result of political considerations became part of the problem. Party bosses diligently sought positions for their political supporters, evident from the beginning of federal control of immigration.[8]

Maud Mosher served as a matron initially in the Ellis Island boarding section and then took an assignment in the temporary detention division from

1903 to 1907. A woman from Kansas, never having worked with immigrants, and knowing little about Ellis Island, she accepted the position out of "a spirit of adventure." Her first impressions are revealing:

> As I stood and watched the immigrants coming in, it looked as though they would never cease . . . 2 Matrons, very grave and dignified, stood there [during the line inspection] looking and occasionally taking some woman or woman and man out of the ranks. Officers at different places giving strange commands in foreign tongues. Little children were crying, tugging at their mother's skirts . . . some of the many babies were screaming. Men and women and children were also bending under burdens which seemed almost beyond their strength to carry bags, bundles, great packs, valises without handles tied together with rope, little tin trunks, great baskets, cooking utensils. . . . So many look weak and starved, so many were filthy and dirty . . . so low and degraded looking, and so poor, so dreadfully poor! And I—I had to stay, I had to stay . . . Every day the terrible feeling of being in a place from which there was no escape grew upon me. The noise and confusion, the curt commands of the officers, the Sundays the same as other days—for the Sabbath is not observed on Ellis Island—the thousands of poor people arriving every day, the misery of the deported. The tears were always so near my eyes that I just had to keep on smiling to keep them from flowing.

She also spoke about the harsh treatment she received from one of her superiors who spoke in "his usual harsh, brutal manner when delivering orders to the matrons."[9]

Frank Martocci, an Ellis Island interpreter and inspector, commented that workers left from the Barge Office at the Battery at 9 o'clock each morning and took the ferry boat to the island; depending on the number of immigrants, they sometimes worked from 9 a.m. to 9 p.m. four days a week. Sympathetic to the immigrants' plight, he nonetheless admitted, "I couldn't help but lose my patience. Waiting for friends, brothers, mothers, fathers, or sisters, they looked at me so hopefully, so anxiously, that my sympathy for them was quite a strain on my nerves." The number of immigrants made the workday hectic and "terribly busy." Nonetheless, he said that "there were many times when an inspector's sympathy was touched, despite the calloused attitude we were forced to adopt as a sort of self-protection."[10]

Commissioner Edward Corsi, looking back at the island's immigration history, admitted that "our immigration officials have not always been as humane as they might have been in dealing with the problems of deportation and divided families." He noted a case in which a Russian Jewish family was unfairly deported although the father had enough money to support his wife and children.[11] Troubles were evident from the first years. Terence Powderly, commissioner-general of immigration from 1897 to 1902, expressed early concerns regarding poor treatment of arrivals and stated that the "discourtesy to those who called to meet their friends on landing were frequent." An investigation in 1900 led to the firing of 11 workers for "offenses such as overcharges for food, misleading immigrants as to destination, procuring admission of friends and relatives to see newly landed immigrants for a fee, overcharges in exchanging foreign for American money, downright cruelty to aliens, petty thievery, and false statements as to distances to be traveled." When William Williams became commissioner of immigration at Ellis Island in 1902, he noted the mistreatment of immigrants he found when taking office. He immediately issued a directive that "immigrants be treated with kindness and civility by everyone at Ellis Island. Neither harsh language nor rough handling will be tolerated."[12] He also stated that those employees who see concessionaires mistreating immigrants and do not report it will be punished. Mistreatment included waiters in the dining room not dealing with the immigrants well. This order's immediacy indicated once again that immigration workers did not always provide the new arrivals with decent treatment.

Ellis Island Concessionaires

Concessionaires who won government contracts provided the food, currency exchange, or baggage transfer services at Ellis Island. These concession contracts were worth a lot of money, but the service provided was not always good or honest. Who received contracts for concessions and money exchange at Ellis Island often became a political decision involving patronage, thereby leaving the system open to corruption. So many immigrants arrived, and so much money could be pilfered by food and currency concessionaires, inspectors, and baggage handlers charging outrageous fees for delivering baggage. With the food concession firm prior to 1905 "food was doled out by helpers regardless of sanitation . . . and immigrants were impressed into the service of serving food."[13] Corsi quoted a passage from an English newspaper from 1901 describing an eyewitness account of a meal being served at Ellis Island: "We passed in a long line around the room. A man with filthy hands filled our hats and handkerchiefs with mouldy prunes. Another thrust two lumps of bread in our hands. Supervising the distribution was a foul mouthed Bowery tough."[14] In 1910, the food concessioner was replaced after the discovery that immigrants were not being suitably fed. Efforts to reform the food service failed and often met with hostile reactions from the food concessionaires' political allies. Commissioner Howe (1914–1919) suggested that the government provide the food rather than private contractors. A congressman, serving as a lawyer for the food company, assailed him as a socialist and radical.

Given the amount of money in question in regard to all Ellis Island functions, opposition to change was always strong from the many companies that profited from the immigration trade, such as railway and steamship companies, hotel owners, baggage concessionaires, and other businesses. Howe claimed that "aliens in this country were losing large sums of money, through irresponsible bankers, with whom they made deposits, bought exchange, or purchased tickets for themselves or their friends." His investigation "unearthed losses of twelve million dollars in a single year in New York alone. The worst offender fled the country as a result of the investigation."[15]

The money exchange concession, for example, earned $25,000 in 1906, and the individual who fed the detainees garnered $65,000. Immigrants could be cheated in many ways, for example, in giving incorrect change to those who bought food. Money exchanges where immigrants changed their foreign currency for American dollars were another place where immigrants could be mistreated. Transactions took place just before leaving the island, and immigrants could be easily cheated because of lack of familiarity with American currency.[16] One individual passing through Ellis Island reported that the exchange had stolen 75 percent of his money. Theodore Lubik, who worked in food service at the island, commented that "people there had the concessions, selling candy, apples, and so on. They're the ones who made the most money." With one eye on the inspectors, they or their helpers cheated the immigrants.[17]

Earlier at Castle Garden, the cheating was at least as bad as occurred at Ellis Island. John Weber, the first commissioner of immigration at Ellis Island, describes the scene at Castle Garden: "After being passed they were turned into an enclosure, then a gate was opened at the farther end admitting a horde of boarding house runners" who then ran "toward the affrighted aliens, calling out their respective boarding houses, pulling and hauling the poor dazed creatures this way and that . . . After herding them in groups they were finally marched off to their temporary quarters where they could be plucked at leisure . . . Such proceedings were the introduction to America . . . also the first glimpse of our ways and manners."[18] Ellis Island had been built partly in an effort to keep immigrants safe from boardinghouse runners, who took them to overpriced boardinghouses and overcharged them for getting there, but problems continued with these runners, as well as with procurers of women for prostitution, various con men, and other crooks. *Collier's* magazine commented that "many of the old schemes of the hawks who prey upon the simple immigrant, the schemes that were used in the old days of Castle Garden, have been revived."[19] Once placed in the boardinghouse, immigrants had difficulty getting out. To deal with the constant assaults immigrants faced as they exited the Barge Office, various immigrant protection societies formed, such as the Society for the Protection of Italian Immigrants, the North American Civic League for Immigrants, HIAS, and others. The New York police started stationing more officers at the barge gate to control the avaricious mob.

Minor thievery took place on Ellis Island as well among workers, including inspectors and concessionaires. A 1902 investigation listed the cases of immigrants robbed at the island. Some of those robbed could have had other immigrants steal their money rather than island staff. Nonetheless, the report claimed that the immigrants, as wards of the government, should have been protected. Some cases, however, did mention Ellis Island staff as the culprits: Gustav Lichtenberger in 1900 had "$5 taken from him by an employee . . . Julius F. von Vesteneck, an Interpreter, recently relieved an immigrant woman of $1, but was permitted to resign instead of being dismissed."[20] These were relatively small amounts, but not for the impoverished new arrivals, who had very little.

Smuggling and Further Corruption

Chinese immigration through San Francisco and later Angel Island had its accusations of corruption as well, and the activity lasted for years. Sometimes corruption was evident among consular or immigration officials and sometimes among the Angel Island staff. In 1906 President Theodore Roosevelt had to step in to deal with corruption, when he eliminated the dishonesty through bribery at the Hong Kong American consulate. Fraud was apparent long before Angel Island was opened. Immigration officials sold papers claiming U.S. residence, and immigrants bribed inspectors and interpreters at various border crossings. One steamship company, so sure of their bribes' effect, assured passengers of successful entry into the United States in the late 1890s. U.S. marshals in 1903, given the job of placing deported Chinese on ships heading back to China, often allowed, for a large fee, the deported immigrants to enter and instead switched them with Chinese who wanted to go back to their homeland.

The mostly Chinese kitchen staff would smuggle messages containing information to help immigrants during questioning. The staff became the conduit between Chinese in San Francisco and their immigrant relatives. Kitchen workers secured messages when they visited certain stores on their days away from the island and then, for a fee, sent the hidden messages to the dining room tables nearest the kitchen and then on to the intended immigrant recipient. Sometimes, the broker arranging the immigration took money from applicants with the excuse that the inspectors and interpreters required a bribe. The broker would keep the money. If the case failed, he would claim that the money given was not sufficient; if the immigrant was accepted, nothing more had to be said. Another example of illegal activities at this station involved John Endicott Gardner, who, along with other interpreters, faced corruption accusations of taking bribes to help immigrants secure acceptance. Accusations against Gardner might have been due to his partial Chinese background since negative stereotyping of the Chinese was endemic in America and in the immigration service at that time, and these bigoted attitudes created a suspicion of the Chinese or mixed-parentage interpreters as being corrupt. Chinese individuals, for example, could not become inspectors, and neither could women. Letting Chinese and Japanese stowaways into the country indicated another aspect of illegal practices. In 1915, U.S. Customs officials, not trusting the immigration staff, searched the ship *Mongolia* and discovered 86 Chinese stowaways. W. H. Tidwell, a special agent of the Customs services, had been warned that this ship had numerous immigrants trying to enter the United States illegally. The tip, in the form of a letter, revealed that "the steamer *Mongolia* has stowaways on board. The No. 1 boatswain has eight of them. Fireman Cheung has 25. The No. 1 Saloon waiter has 20. The Chief Engineer gets $100.00 (gold) for each one." The problem was not with the immigration staff in this situation, but with the ship's crew. The *Mongolia* event was not unique.[21]

The *Mongolia* incident led to numerous investigations of the immigration staff and the crew of incoming ships. In 1916, immigration officials discovered another occurrence also on an anonymous tip as revealed in an investigation; investigators accused Under Clerk Presley A. McFarland of taking files out of the records room for the purpose of altering them. He named others involved in the unlawful activities: "Junior Clerk (Stenographer and Typist) Robert Fergusson, Under Clerk William Armstrong, Junior Watchman Theodore Kaplan, and former Under Clerk Agathon Hilkemeyer." The investigation further led to Angel Island lawyers, interpreters, and inspectors. The charge stated that files had been stolen, changed, and used to bring in illegal immigrants. Lawyers bribed immigration staff to secure a positive inspection of their clients. The lead inspector, special agent for the U.S. Labor Department John B. Densmore, noted in his 1917 report to the secretary of labor that "fraud in connection with examinations manifests itself in the employment of fake witnesses and affidavits; the surreptitious coaching of applicants, by means of letters secretly delivered to them in the detention quarters of the Immigration Station; purposely easy examinations on the part of the inspectors; underhanded assistance rendered applicants, during the course of examinations, by the official Chinese interpreters; changing of notes on the part of stenographers who report the hearings; reconciling discrepancies in testimony by the inspectors who conduct the examinations."[22] The investigation culminated in the firing of the involved clerks, stenographers, watchmen, interpreters, and inspectors. The Densmore report further led to charges against lawyers, previous employees, photographers, forgers, and Chinese contact men in their community. The law firm most involved in bribery and perjury could no longer deal with any matter concerning the immigration process. According to the Densmore report, the main law firm, which bribed seven inspectors, was responsible for 2,734 Chinese immigrant entries from 1913 to 1916.[23] One year later Densmore stated that San Francisco was still the main port for smuggling immigrants into America and that those involved secured large amounts of money yearly.

Angel Island inspector John Birge Sawyer, concentrating on Chinese immigration, noted how the *Mongolia* and later incidents apparently had an impact on all the inspectors. He wrote that only 4 of 11 inspectors remained after the investigation. He felt that the investigation had imparted a negative label to all inspectors, even to those who felt that the exclusion laws were unjust. Sawyer observed that "the expulsion of officers and disbarment of attorneys and indictment of many connected with Chinese immigration is having its results in demoralization of the immigration game." Upon receiving a new appointment elsewhere, he commented, "I feel much relieved to be done with the Station. It is not a safe place to be connected with and I feel that I will have to be pretty desperate to return to it . . . I see only stormy seas ahead for them and consequently for the Service."[24]

Similarly, an instance of corruption at Ellis Island allowed steerage passengers in 1901 to buy falsified citizenship papers from corrupt ship officials and immigrant inspectors who boarded the ship before reaching port. These immigrants could then go right into New York as citizens without first stopping at Ellis Island. One estimate is that 10,000 immigrants had come into the United States over a few years in this manner. Captain John Halpin took immigrants illegally off the island after dark in 1901 and brought them into New York for 50 cents each.[25] Taking bribes to allow immigrants into the country as citizens became an ongoing problem. According to Edward Steiner, an American who studied immigration by traveling as a steerage immigrant a number of times, an inspector told him he would have problems in being accepted unless he paid the inspector a bribe. Steiner also mentioned a Bohemian girl who was guaranteed acceptance if she met the inspector at a hotel afterward. She was mortified and asked Steiner, "Do I look like that?"[26]

In 1921, commissioner of immigration Frederick A. Wallis, outraged by immigrant accusations of being cheated on the island, fired a dozen inspectors, interpreters, and watchmen and suspended Augustus Schell, head of the law division, pending an investigation. The charges involved stealing baggage, taking bribes, and admitting immigrants for a fee. The treasurer's office also had been consistently missing money. The situation went on for a while since no one had checked the cash flow for years. Wallis said, "I'm going to break up the rotten state of affairs on Ellis Island if it ruins me. The public doesn't realize how bad conditions have been. People have been robbed here as if they were children. It is the easiest thing in the world to rob them."[27]

Years earlier, President Roosevelt tried to rid the immigration depot of corrupt and offensive officials, including the assistant commissioner Edward F. McSweeney in 1902, but corruption continued. McSweeney, although politically protected, eventually was forced to resign. John Lederhilger, one of McSweeney's aides and Registry Division boss, had, among other offenses, forced immigrant women to answer lewd questions, and he molested some of them. Improving the caliber of officials proved difficult since many were well connected politically. Roosevelt had to fight his own Republican Party to get rid of McSweeney. The political connections of some corrupt individuals were strong, especially within the New York Republican Party and with the steamship companies. Furthermore, McSweeney held a civil service position, although initially a patronage appointment, and Roosevelt faced protests in removing such a staff member.

In 1902, Roosevelt appointed attorney William Williams as commissioner of immigration as part of a contemplated major reform effort at Ellis Island. Roosevelt urged a reluctant Williams to take the position because so many immigrants were arriving through the station and "were being improperly inspected, robbed, and abused."[28] The new commissioner found numerous illegal practices: unqualified persons conducting immigrant inspections, politicians and immigration officials interfering with Boards of Special Inquiry, bribery, unclean dining rooms and inadequate food handling, and immigrants with large amounts of cash being taken to the chief inspector for personal interrogation and fleecing. Williams's friends, put into the inspection line pretending to be immigrants, exposed the corrupt officials.

The commissioner's work involved many problems and difficult decisions. Hundreds of thousands of immigrants had to be landed and processed, and the newspapers constantly watched the procedure to see that all took place with a careful hand. Williams also had to deal with political critics, and he became immediately part of the continuous discussion on whether and how many immigrants should be allowed into the United States. The forces on both sides of the discussion had strong and vocal opinions, ranging from those who wanted to curtail immigration further to those who wanted few laws restricting immigration. Commissioners often faced criticism from all sides of the immigration issue, as well as from congressional advocates for one position or the other. Any decision made in relation to immigration had its detractors.[29] Williams's successor, Robert Watchorn (1905–1909), mentioned that every morning he received mail from two groups: the first protested that he was not strict enough in following the immigration laws, and the other criticized him for being too severe with the same laws. If inspectors rejected too many immigrants, the factory owners who needed laborers complained; if inspectors accepted too many immigrants, the labor unions grumbled because of the competition from these new workers. Newspapers kept up a steady stream of both negative and positive comments on the station.

Who received concession contracts remained a constant issue, with most contracts being awarded to those with friends in the New York Republican Party. Williams made a valiant attempt to improve conditions on the island but found that politically shielded officials—in one case even his own assistant, who Roosevelt safeguarded—and protected concessionaires were difficult to remove. The food concessionaire, for example, actually worked for a previous Republican district leader, who was making enormous profits from a poorly run service. Williams had to constantly struggle against political interference on every matter, even the proposed promotion of a gateman to an inspector. He had to explain to a New York senator that the promotion would not take place since the individual was "not fitted either by temperament or training" for an inspector's position.[30] Politicians continually asked for favors for friends and constituents. Williams, trying to reform the station and deal with these problems, issued a statement to island staff in 1903 that "swindling immigrants is contemptible business and whoever does this, under whatever form, should be despised" and will face serious consequences.[31]

When taking on the concessionaires initially, Williams received praise from the *Commercial Advertiser*, which said that he had "broken up a nest of patronage that has long been perpetuated there, and which for years has been a smoldering public scandal."[32] Other reforms indicate the situation before he arrived: detention forms had to be filled out in ink so unauthorized changes could not be made, a crackdown on shipping companies that purposely landed individuals who had excludable illnesses, no more free passes from railroads to immigration personnel, and steamship companies being emphatically told to improve the ship manifest system by making sure they did the manifests correctly. Fines enforced the correct procedure. His effort over a number of years to dismiss his assistant and Roosevelt's friend, Joe Murray, finally led to Williams's resignation. The president would not budge on his protection of Murray.

Corruption, difficult to curtail, always returned. Immigrants deported at Ellis Island did not always stay deported. In 1904, Williams complained that excluded immigrants placed on ships set to sail the next morning sometimes escaped owing to bribes given to the ship's crew. He said that "the temptation to connive to escape, especially if the person ordered deported has money and friends to go to in this city, is very great."[33] These escapes apparently happened often and did not cease. Williams in 1910, during his second tenure as commissioner, brought charges against the Hellenic Transatlantic Steam Navigation Company for sneaking sick immigrants into the country for a fee. Fifteen company officials went to jail. In 1912 Williams charged one immigrant official on the island with extorting money from immigrants allowed to enter under bond. How many immigrants came into the country in these ways remains unknown, but corruption had occurred over a number of years. Some inspectors would make it easier to get through the examination line if given a bribe. Or, as Dr. Robert Leslie, an Ellis Island medical officer from 1912 to 1914, related, "politicians . . . had names of people that they wanted to have no examinations," and these immigrants were allowed to go through. Henry H. Curran, immigrant commissioner at Ellis Island from 1923 to 1926, complained that an influential cabinet member in the Harding administration strongly pressed Curran to allow an individual suspected of smuggling immigrants into the country for a fee to take charge of the money exchange office on the island. The individual's qualifications rested on his assistance with the Italian vote in the 1920 presidential election. Curran refused, but the political pressures from politicians of both parties stayed constant.[34]

Investigations continued into the 1930s and later. Secretary of Labor Frances Perkins issued a report in 1935 on a fraud investigation at Ellis Island. The inquiry "uncovered evidence of systematic fraud in immigration and naturalization cases in the New York district perpetuated over a period of years by racketeers acting in collusion with employees of this Service." The following gives a more in-depth account of the crimes uncovered in the investigation:

> Manifests had been altered, official documents were missing and files had been stolen . . . It had been ascertained that up to $100 had been paid in naturalization cases involving false witnesses or the passing of applicants unqualified, and that from $300 to $1200 had been collected for the alteration of manifests to show legal entry . . . It is believed that they may have aggregated $1,000,000. The lion's share was retained by racketeers and crooked attorneys and agents who solicited business and were in direct contact with the aliens concerned, while the remainder was paid to employees whose connivance was essential. By the close of the fiscal year, 1,600 alleged illegal entry cases had been investigated, with 424 arrests and 83 deportations, 34 indictments had been obtained in fraudulent naturalizations, 200 cases had been prepared in cancellation of citizenship, and 29 cases against employees.

Those involved included lawyers, agents, and Ellis Island employees. And again in 1940, investigations implicated lawyers, government workers, steamship agents, and immigrant consultants in fraud.[35]

Sometimes medical officers or contract labor inspectors took bribes. An immigrant diagnosed with measles or another contagious disease would be told that deportation would occur unless a bribe was given. After hospitalization and now disease free, the immigrant could enter the country, as he would have been able to anyway with the disease cured. However, immigrants could be easily fooled into thinking that the bribe was the main factor in entry in these cases.[36] Immigrants coming from countries where bribery was a way of life in dealing with government officials never knew whether offering a bribe would lead to exclusion or get them accepted faster. Of course, corrupt officials asked for a bribe rather than waiting for it to be offered. For example, in 1921, acting assistant surgeon Challis H. Dawson requested a bribe of $400 to exempt from more intensive medical examination the fiancée of an Italian man already in New York. Dawson lost his job as a result of his corrupt behavior.[37] Furthermore, not all inspectors were legitimate. Someone could easily secure an inspector's uniform, come to Ellis Island by ferry, and extort or swindle money from immigrants at his leisure and then disappear. One Polish immigrant was so swindled when a man dressed as an inspector asked to see his money and took a $50 bill from him, claiming that it was counterfeit.[38]

Although most missionary and immigrant aid societies did honest and excellent work, some societies caused problems if they misrepresented themselves. Commissioner Williams banned all individuals from the Lutheran Immigrant Home in 1902 because their purpose was clearly commercial rather than religious or beneficent. In a letter to Rev. H. J. Berkemeier, Williams wrote, "You were allowed the freedom of this island under the supposition that your only object was to assist immigrants . . . now I have conclusive proof that instead of assisting immigrants you are in the habit of actually preventing recently arrived girls of meeting their friends and of compelling them to accept employment against their will with people who have previously directed you to look up servants for them at Ellis Island."[39]

Improvements made in subsequent years eliminated, through further expulsions, some corruption. In 1909, Williams told the St. Joseph's Home for the Protection of Polish Immigrants and the Swedish Immigrant Home that they could no longer have representatives on the island. The complaint against the Polish society, for example, involved a claim, soon verified, that they charged the immigrants for food after stating that food was free and also charged a fee to those who wished to hire the immigrants. Furthermore, the aid societies did not give the immigrants help in getting to their destinations as they claimed to be doing. Williams banned the Austrian Society of

New York in 1910 from boarding immigrants after the North American Civic League for Immigrants sent an agent to secretly investigate their facility. The agent reported that "the beds she [the agent] slept in had vermin and the mattress and bed clothing were filthy in the extreme," and the men who worked there were vulgar in their treatment of the female immigrants.[40] Williams's 1910 investigation of immigrant aid organizations stated that he "found that the trustees of some (not all) of these societies had confided the management to incompetent or corrupt underlings . . . Some of these practices included housing them [immigrants] in quarters of extreme filth . . . exposing girls to coarse, vulgar treatment, turning them over to improper persons, and reporting fictitious addresses as to where they were sent, treating immigrants in an unfriendly, even brutal manner, taking their money on deposit and refusing to surrender it on request," among other offenses.[41] On other occasions, after Commissioner Wallis's investigation in 1921, Italian and Jewish societies dismissed one worker each for taking money from immigrants. In the case of HIAS, considered one of the best agencies on the island, the social worker had received money in order to file an appeal. Even honest, effective aid organizations had their corrupt employees.[42]

Furthermore, situations occurred in which individuals, who actually worked for boardinghouses, directed immigrants to those locations, sometimes posing as representatives of missionary or immigrant aid societies. Law firms that stationed personnel at Ellis Island indicated corrupt practices at times and provided immigrants with misinformation for an often exorbitant fee. In some cases, lawyers could be barred from dealing with any immigrant matter at any U.S. entry/processing point. In the period from August 1904 to October 1908, about 25 lawyers were barred from working with immigrants. One case involved an Italian immigrant who had been charged a high fee for getting his son cleared for entry well after the son had been sent back to the Old World.[43] Some law firms advertised falsely in the foreign language press that they could secure easy entry through Ellis Island. Some immigrants had legal help from compatriots to protect them; unscrupulous lawyers targeted others.

Immigrants, upon leaving the island and after going to the Barge Office on the New York mainland to pick up baggage, found themselves released into a mob of individuals bent on cheating and swindling them in one way or another. Sometimes the baggage concessionaire was the problem. Barney Biglin, with Republican connections, had control of the baggage concession at Castle

Garden and early on at Ellis Island. Found to be charging too much, he lost the contract, but he secured aspects of the concession again in 1905 and became the main concessionaire in 1908, transporting immigrants and their baggage from the Barge Office to New York's Grand Central Station supposedly using wagons and offering a seat for each immigrant. Allowed to charge 50 cents, he instead took the immigrants on the subway for 5 cents a person and kept the rest. Biglin and his colleague made millions in this fashion. Efforts to dislodge Biglin from this contract failed until 1911. Although Commissioner Watchorn considered him and his partner "a couple of 'importunate and contentious leeches,'" he could not get rid of Biglin owing to "an army of politicians" who protected him.[44] Baggage corruption did not end with Biglin.

Railroads could also be a problem for immigrants traveling inland. In 1903, Commissioner Williams reported that the railroads were sending immigrants by an overly lengthy route that forced them "to buy baskets of food in New York City at most exorbitant rates." Ellis Island officials sent Philip Cowen, an immigration inspector working particularly with Jewish immigrants, to investigate the rail service. Traveling undercover as an immigrant going from the island to Pennsylvania Station and then to Philadelphia, he discovered that the immigrants received poor treatment. Rail agents often charged immigrants first-class fares for second-class service. The rail cars set aside for immigrants were not kept clean and had insufficient toilet space. The service provided made for unnecessarily long and delayed trips. Furthermore, the rail officials initially gave free passes to immigration officials. Steamship companies engaged in similar activities, all in an effort to secure easier access to and acceptance of immigrants, which would benefit their companies.[45]

The immigrant aid societies did protect many immigrants at the island and also at the New York pier from this crowd of cheats, but they could only do so much. Brandenburg relates one incident in which an immigrant was taken to the pier and put into a carriage to go to the railroad station. The carriage driver asked for a certain fee, which the immigrant paid. The carriage driver then stopped when out of sight from the pier and the aid societies and asked for more money, and again the immigrant paid. He then stopped again in a few minutes and asked for still more money. In this way a newcomer could be cheated when first arriving. This situation happened often.

Commissioner Wallis in 1921 noted his concern with grafting among boardinghouse runners and cab drivers, not to mention the usual pickpockets who plied their trade among the immigrant crowd. Some went to Ellis Island on the ferry carrying relatives. As a *New York Times* article relates in July 1921, "Last week a man was picked up by one of the inspectors who was selling alleged Board of Special Inquiry passes."[46] It was easy to cheat the newly arrived immigrants, unfamiliar with American customs and not able to speak English.[47]

Labor Issues

Beyond corruption issues, Ellis Island workers could also be subject to basic labor demands obvious among American employees generally. Matrons complained in 1914 that they were doing more than caring for detained women and children, "which involve[s] constant exposure to disease and constant nervous strain." Extra duties, including interpreting for inspectors and working seven days a week, offered no extra compensation. The matrons wanted raises and better working conditions. During World War I, the number of workers decreased with the lower number of immigrants. Some shipping lines with enemy ties, such as North German Lloyd, no longer came to the island. In 1914, Ellis Island allowed into the United States about 878,000 immigrants; by 1919, the number had dropped to about 27,000. Employees became concerned about job retention, but also about the workforce reduction taking place just prior to an expected immigration increase at war's end. Having gone through years of long work hours and reaching a point where the inspection process had been made as efficient as possible, the staff objected to the immigration officials' lack of foresight. Commissioner Howe in 1914 agreed and sent the workers' appeal to the secretary of labor. The secretary rejected the appeal. Howe commented in 1915 that "the furloughs and transfers directed by the department have to a great extent impaired the efficiency of the Ellis Island force . . . Should immigration materially increase . . . it will require considerable time to restore the personnel to its former degree of efficiency."[48]

Detentions declined as well, but as Commissioner Howe said in 1916, the immigrants faced longer detentions, partly because of the inability to send them back to their homelands during the war. Ellis Island became a prison for these people, and their behavior deteriorated. Howe complained that he needed more security personnel. Those at their jobs stayed there for many hours and through promised vacations. He asked the commissioner-general of immigration to hire more watchmen or transfer those moved to the Mexican border back to Ellis Island.[49] In 1920, engineers, firemen, electricians, and various other physical plant workers warned of a strike if a wage increase demand could not be met. Workers had been promised raises that had not been forthcoming. The strike did not occur only because the Philadelphia immigration commissioner traveled to the island and pledged that higher wages would be secured soon. This issue did not disappear, and requests for higher wages continued. In 1922, immigration commissioner Robert E. Tod wrote to the commissioner-general of immigration in Washington, D.C., that "all of the employees [underlining in original] at Ellis Island are grossly underpaid."[50]

Lack of sufficient workers to handle the immigrant flood continued throughout the heavy immigration years. A funding shortage and understaffing existed owing to long-term budget shortages. The budget shortfalls might have been one of the factors leading to the continuous corruption issues through the years. The deficiencies certainly led to overcrowding as a constant complaint at the island. Into the 1920s, according to the Department of Labor, certain inadequate conditions remained: scarcity of space in sleeping and dining areas, poor facilities in areas for women and children, lack of separate quarters "for criminal and immoral classes who have either been detained or are awaiting deportation," more recreational areas and places for detained immigrants separate from sleeping sections, "proper segregation with recreational facilities for diseased aliens who are being treated in hospitals," and segregation from immigrants detained for mental considerations.[51]

Regardless of the source of corruption or the conditions on the island, the impact could be significant. As Commissioner Tod remarked, "If we sleep immigrants on cold tiled floors without covering, give them impure food, rob them, curse them and handle them worse than cattle, then they go out into the nation and practice just what they have received here on the island. Ellis Island is not only the 'gateway of the nation' but it is the nation's kindergarten of Americanization, and what they receive on the island is what they will live out in the nation." He continued, "Let the immigrant know that his work is appreciated, that this Government is his friend and that this country is his opportunity, then and only then will the foreigner make his best contribution to our American life and labor."[52]

5 How Immigrants Responded to Entering America and Changed the System

FINALLY ACCEPTED at Ellis Island and entering America—how did that feel? Did expectations fit the reality seen? Did immigrants believe that the country welcomed them? If so, why did Congress pass strong restrictionist legislation in the 1920s? Immigrants saw a bewildering country where their success and prospects remained in doubt. Those accepted would go to New York by ferry or be escorted to railway stations on barges. As they went into the city or further inland, reactions ranged over the emotional spectrum from joy to fear to sadness to anticipation, or all these sensations at once.

Louis Adamic, who had a last-minute harrowing experience with the inspector, describes his departure from Ellis Island: "I laughed, perhaps a bit hysterically, as the little Ellis Island ferryboat bounded over the rough, white-capped waters of the bay toward the Battery . . . I was in New York—in America."[1]

"They used to tell us on the other side that the trains in America ran on rooftops," said Arnold Weiss, who came to America in 1921 from Russia. Immigrants experienced amazement at the elevated railroad lines that crossed the city. "To us it was magic! We had never seen anything like it," Weiss continued. William Reinhart from Germany, who arrived in New York in 1910 at age 4, also was astonished by the elevated trains. "Then we got on an elevated subway train and, all of a sudden, we were in the sky. Here we were twenty-one days on the water, and now we were sailing through the sky with water underneath us." New York's hectic lifestyle and tall buildings fascinated others. Ida Levy, arriving from Russia in 1921, remembered seeing "the rushing people, the trains, people rushing to the trains. And the buildings—I couldn't look up to the top of them. In my city, I never saw an extra person. I never saw a train." Abraham Livshein, coming to America from Poland in 1921 at age 18, found himself awed by the lights blinking on the river at night. "I never saw electric light. The only light we had was a kerosene lamp. But now there were red lights and green lights and bright lights blinking, and little boats." He was particularly impressed, as were other immigrants, by the Lipton's coffee and tea billboard. "We couldn't get over it, there was flashing like giant hand-writing in the sky . . . That was a marvel I never even dreamt of." Michael Pappas, arriving from Greece in 1913, said he was astounded when he saw the city "because I was brought up in a small village, I didn't know much about big buildings." He also admitted that he and the four other Greeks arriving with him expressed fear since they had "no money . . . only sixteen years old, the first time I was out of my home," and no place to live. Morris Shapiro from Russia, entering in 1923, had his ship sidetracked to Providence, Rhode Island, because of overcrowding at the New York port. His examination took place in Providence, and since he had paid to go to New York, he received a free boat ticket to travel there. Seeing Providence first did not diminish his surprise at New York. "I shall never forget the astonishment I felt at my first glimpse of this great city. I was bewildered at the sight of trains running overhead, under my very feet, trolleys clanging, thousands upon thousands of taxis tearing around corners, and millions of people rushing and pushing through the screaming noise day in and day out. To me this city appeared as a tremendous overstuffed roar, where people just burst with a desire to live."[2]

Nils Sablin, arriving from Sweden in 1921, did not feel so enchanted with New York: "I could not get over the dirty tenements and the houses so packed in together. Some of the people did not look so prosperous, and I wondered if America was so wonderful after all that I had heard about it."[3] Arnold Weiss came to America with his mother, but he also found that its streets were not paved with gold. His mother remarried, and when Arnold reached 13, his stepfather no longer wanted to support him. His mother said, "But you promised me, when I married you, you'd take care of my child. You're going back on your word! He said, Well, how long do you think I can support him!" So Arnold left home to avoid more family fights about him and looked for a job. "So I went out peddling with shoelaces, with cottons, and with handkerchiefs. On weekends, I traveled the trains selling the weekend newspapers and in such a way I got my support. It started with three dollars a week and went up to seven dollars a week."[4] Edward Corsi spoke of his surprise and in some matters disappointment with America:

> I liked the din and bustle, the hurrying crowds on every hand, but I could see that my mother was bewildered. They were in startling contrast to the peaceful routine of life back in the Abruzzi. It had never occurred to me that any language except Italian was spoken anywhere . . . Here there were strange tongues on every side. I began to feel dazed and lost, but it gave me a new grip on myself to arrive in Harlem's little Italy and see and hear all about me people of my own nationality. Our new home was a disappointment . . . here we found ourselves paying what seemed like an enormous price for four sordid tenement rooms . . . My mother was discouraged by the sight of the apartment the moment she stepped into it, and she never overcame the repulsion . . . She was never happy here and, though she tried, could not adjust herself to the poverty and despair in which we had to live . . . My stepfather had no special training . . . and had to take employment at manual labor in a piano factory. He earned eleven dollars a week which was barely enough to keep our bodies and souls together . . . There were many times when we had nothing to eat in the house. There was one period when my stepfather was out of work for eighteen months.

Walter Mrozowski from Poland, landing about 1906, spoke of his immediate need to find a job after leaving the boat: "There was no one to help me. I was a young fellow with no relatives or friends I could call on. It was a rough spot I was in, but I made up my mind I would make the best of it. I could not go back to Poland as I did not have the money to buy a ticket. So I walked around New York for the rest of the day. As night came on, I felt tired and sleepy but I knew I could not spend any money for a hotel room." He finally fell asleep in a freight train that began to move. He woke up much later when the train stopped in Torrington, Connecticut. He finally found a job there and stayed.[5]

Irene Meladaki Zambelli, arriving in 1914 from Greece, went to a rail station and waited for a few hours. She then got on the train with other immigrants. "We had not the slightest idea where we were going." After three full days on the train with numerous changes, she arrived in New Orleans, where family met her. Her cousin, however, tried and failed to get a job. Speaking only Greek, he finally joined the military and found himself back in Europe as a soldier in the U.S. Army.[6]

Rachel Goldman, a minor from Bialystock, a city in Poland then occupied by the German army, was on the way to Evanston, Illinois, in 1916 and found help from the Travelers' Aid Society. When she arrived in Chicago, the society connected her with relatives. As she said, "Because I was a minor, the Travelers' Aid Society had to take care of me to see that I met the right people." But her relatives had difficulty locating her. "The fellow who had sent the telegram to Evanston from Ellis Island hadn't mentioned in it what train or what railroad I was coming on, and my cousin was telling me what a time they had for two days calling every railroad and finding out if I was on it. I was on a train that took such a long time, being sidetracked all the time for regular trains."[7] Not all immigrants had safe journeys. The same coterie of thieves, procurers, and others who preyed on the immigrants at the Battery in New York also worked the trains and rail stations.

Angel Island Reactions

The Asians entering through Angel Island had different emotions. The attempt to exclude Asians, especially Chinese, their harsh treatment during their detention, and the discrimination against them in America stayed with them for years. Angel Island memories remained bitter. Tet Yee revisited Angel Island many years after admission and wrote,

> I cannot forget my imprisonment in the wooden building,
> The writing on the wall terrifies me,
> Returning here after forty-four years,
> I seek out poems now incomplete.
> But still I remember the memories of sadness, anger, and frustration,
> Memories we have kept from our children.
> The memories are etched in my bones and in my heart.
> Today we can stand proud as Chinese Americans,
> But I will never forget what happened here on Angel Island.
> Where our pain was carved in silence.[8]

Understanding America

Adjustment to American culture could be difficult. Learning English in the schools or in adult education classes became a necessity for survival. Immigrants found that understanding American ways became important. Estelle Schwartz Belford, arriving from Rumania in 1905 at age 5, spoke of her father's adjustment: "My father knew very little of the customs of America . . . When he started working, at the end of the week they gave him his check . . . and he didn't know what that was. He was ashamed to ask because whatever you asked you felt foolish. But he kept it. He thought it was a ticket of some kind. He waited about a month or so and he wasn't getting any money. Finally, he asked somebody and then he realized that piece of paper is really money."[9]

Immigration Surge after World War I and Quota Laws

Right after World War I ended, the migration picked up again and finally led to the passage of new laws to curtail immigration. But before these laws passed, Ellis Island's staff was overwhelmed. Secretary of Labor William B. Wilson assessed the situation at the station in a 1920 report: "Immigration at Ellis Island has nearly reached its pre-war magnitude, and in addition the present law requires the Immigration Service to examine hundreds of thousands of seamen at the Port of New York annually, which is a duty that did not devolve upon the Service in pre-war times." Wilson called for more inspectors, stenographers, clerks, typists, interpreters, watchmen, messengers, and switchboard operators. Staff from other immigration stations had to be transferred to Ellis Island.[10] With immigration increasing, the concern over inadequate numbers of workers intensified. Lack of funding and lack of eligible prospects on the civil service lists led to shortages. Commissioner Tod (1921–1923) observed that many workers were doing the work of two or three people. Turnover at the station meant that, at times, immigrant officials hired inexperienced staff to fill positions. While immigration surged after World War I, the staff was cut by 8 percent in 1921.

The immigration quota laws passed in the 1920s, culminating with the 1924 National Origins Act and its 1929 finalization, did not change the first-sight experiences for immigrants allowed into the United States, but immigration into Ellis and Angel Islands eventually slowed considerably as a result of these laws and the economic collapse of the Great Depression. The laws' intent was to maintain the United States as an Anglo-Saxon nation, and Congress particularly designed this legislation to suppress migration from eastern and southern Europe, largely curtail Asian immigration, and favor those from traditional northern and western European areas. President Calvin Coolidge's essay, with the heading "Whose Country Is This?" and written a few years before he assumed the presidency and signed the 1924 immigration act, readily indicated his eugenic and nativist intentions. He expressed a preference for Nordic immigrants and displeasure at the idea of intermarriage among Nordics and so-called inferior groups, which would lead to substandard progeny.[11]

Initially the 1921 quota law resulted in a sometimes ridiculous but also an intense and poignant rush to Ellis Island. Ships arriving from Europe and Asia tried to arrive in the United States at the beginning of each month and in the first five months of each year so as to avoid being over the quota limit for that month or year. This effort strained the staff's ability to process the immigrants and put most work into the early part of each month. Then, the rest of the month the station was virtually empty, and the staff had little to do. The general procedure established earlier changed. The Great Hall was now used for the Special Inquiry division and for detainees. After 1924 most medical inspections occurred first at the U.S. consulate in the immigrant's home country. This method provided for a more thorough examination and ended the controversy over whether the inspection line exam was too superficial. For these immigrants, their only other scrutiny came just before boarding the ship. However, immigrants could take up to four months after securing a visa (and receiving their most intensive exam) to finally board a ship. The pre-boarding checkup was cursory, and every possibility existed that immigrants could contract a disease in the interim. The next exam occurred on the ship when it reached New York Harbor, but those who were sick, whose status was not clear, or who did not have the funds required to enter would still be sent to Ellis Island. Those immigrants questionable in any way or coming from countries that did not do pre-boarding inspections also went to Ellis Island. This consulate exam reduced the number of immigrants examined and rejected at the island. Owing to monthly quotas, the new system also regulated the number of immigrants entering the United States, especially those intending to emigrate from southern and eastern Europe. However, immigration still flowed from Canada and Mexico. North, South, and Central American immigrants were not part of the quota limitations. The change also meant that pathetic scenes of immigrants denied entry after their arduous sea journey would be limited.

Overseas, Public Health doctors gave the medical examination to the majority of immigrants, but this practice also meant a more intensive exam for those who had not been prescreened when they arrived at Ellis Island. As a result, although the immigrant numbers decreased after the quota laws and doctors inspected fewer at the island stations, the immigrants certified with signs of having tuberculosis or venereal disease increased. As the Surgeon General's report stated in 1925, "It appears that in 1925 as compared to 1914 the efficiency in detecting the presence of the disease called 'the great white plague' [tuberculosis] in aliens seeking admission to the United States was as 20 is to 1. Assuming that the proportion per thousand arrivals who were actually infected with tuberculosis of the lungs was exactly the same in 1914 as in 1925, if the same thoroughness of examination could have been applied in 1914 as was applied in 1925, the United States would have been saved giving domicile to 433 tuberculosis aliens."[12]

Henry Curran served as commissioner from 1923 to 1926, when the quota laws were in effect. The yearly quota ended June 30 of each year and started over on July 1. By June, the quota for most nationalities for the preceding year had been met, so the ships waited for the new quota year. Also, monthly quotas on the total number of immigrants who could arrive affected all immigrants, even those from favored countries.

Curran commented that "on the night before the first of July there were twenty ships down the bay, loaded with 10,000 immigrants and waiting for the minute of midnight to dash across the entry line," an invisible line that the immigration service had set in the bay. "So the laden ships, coming into port through the last days of June, had to lie at anchor and wait, in Gravesend Bay outside the line. If they should cross the line before midnight of June 30, though it were only by a second, their immigrant cargoes would be charged to the old year, which had no quotas left, and sent back to the countries 'whence they came' at the expense of the steamship companies—deported. No ship was going to risk an inspector's stop watch finding it inside the line before midnight!" So the ships at midnight dashed forward, trying to beat the other ships, before the quota was met for that year. If an immigrant sailed on the last ship, it surely meant deportation for being over quota and thus being sent back to the old country. Curran expressed his sentiments on this situation: "Day by day, the barges took them from Ellis Island back to the ships again, back to the ocean, back to—what? As they trooped aboard the big barges under my window, carrying their heavy bundles, some in their quaint, colorful native costumes worn to celebrate their first glad day in free America, some carrying little American flags, most of them quietly weeping, they twisted something in my heart that hurts to this day."[13]

In one particularly odd case, which indicated the bureaucratic foolishness that could result in a too close interpretation of the quota laws, a Swedish ship carrying Finns had crossed the line slightly before midnight to avoid hitting another ship. As a result, the ship's bow was coming in on the previous month's quota and the stern on the new month's quota. Finnish immigrants in the stern of the ship secured admittance within the September quota for Finland, while those in the bow faced deportation because the bow came in a few seconds earlier while still August, with that month's quota already filled. These immigrants, not knowing how to answer the inspector's question of whether they congregated in the stern or bow of the ship, decided that to say they were rushing into America and therefore resided in the bow was the right answer. Unfortunately, this meant that they had to go back to Finland and reenter the next month.[14]

Sometimes, as in the early days of intensive medical exams, one member of a family had to go back as inspectors admitted the others. After the quota laws passed, if "a part of a family," as Curran relates, "had been born in a country with a quota still open, while the other part had been born in a country whose quota was exhausted, the law let in the first part and deported the other part. Mothers were torn from children, husbands from wives. The law came down like a sword between them, the wide ocean suddenly separated them." In one case a Polish mother, returning to America from a non-quota short trip to Poland to see her sick parents, faced a situation where her baby, born on the ship, could be excluded because the Polish quota was filled. Curran managed to get the baby accepted with some fast-thinking legal tricks.[15]

Occasionally inspectors gave immigrants the choice of going back or extensive detentions. At all processing centers, arrivals found difficulty with the quota laws. An Angel Island social worker in 1937 commented that "to be denied admission and to be deported or kept in detention for months, was like a death-blow to hope and caused them to cry out in despair, 'we have nothing to go back to—nothing, nothing.' "[16]

Sometimes, a sympathetic official could circumvent the quota law. Curran relates the story of one Hungarian girl at Ellis Island whom he came upon "pleading with the inspectors to be admitted. She was alone, and the tears were coming. The inspectors were sorry but helpless, for the quota was exhausted." However, the girl had a violin, and Curran asked her to play something, without saying why. She played well, and Curran "turned to the inspectors. 'Artist, don't you think?' I asked vaguely, winking one eye. 'Exemption—perhaps?' "[17] Apparently artists were non-quota immigrants, and inspectors could consider this girl as such. She was admitted.

Curran spoke of one other way the quotas could be bypassed. Immigrant women on Ellis Island could enter if they married an American citizen, and apparently many men were interested. Curran reports that he received a sudden surge of letters requesting wives. Here is one such letter, reprinted in Curran's memoirs:

> I thought I would write this to you, knowing that you may be able to help me find a life Mate. I am ann American 50 but look 30 . . . and offel lonesome being that I do not run round, like other Men, and so I can not come in contack with any one; and I feel I could not make a wife of the woman of today, they expect so much of a poor Man. I have a small home which I keep all alone, now what I want to know if you have any poor lonesome woman there. I don't care what nation she is as long as she would make a good wife. I would gladly call at your office and marry the same. I would perfur a short heavy-set woman, but I would take any if I could. I have often read of them being sent back, on account of no one to take them here, and I thought I would pen this, I think you will know what I mean, as I feel a peasant woman of the old world would make a better wife to a poor Man than these here. Would you kindly let me know if you can spare One, I would be offel obliged to you. hoping to hear from you soon.[18]

The suitor's fate and his efforts to secure a wife remain unknown.

Impact of Depression

As immigration numbers further declined, so did the number of workers on the islands. The 1930s saw cuts in salaries and hours for staff; however, work actually increased owing to the numbers of immigrants being deported during the Depression years.

By the 1930s the Depression, along with the quota laws, had decreased the number of entries to the point where more people left the United States than arrived. The Depression had forced some immigrants onto public charity and, if within their probationary period, made them liable to deportation.

In Detroit, as in other urban locales, city officials worked with immigration authorities to rid their area of destitute immigrants. And some immigrants even desired deportation during the difficult economic times. Immigrants destitute and within the probationary period could be sent back to their home country with the United States paying for the voyage. At various times, approximately 200 a month registered for voluntary deportation. The *New York Times* wrote in 1933 that "those speaking English were frank about their happiness at the prospect of returning home, explaining that 'on the other side' the lot of the poor was happier." In 1932, 103,295 individuals left America and 35,576 arrived. Of the number leaving, 19,420 were deportations. Again in 1933, a large deportation occurred. Edward Corsi remarked that now "deportation was the big business at Ellis Island," a situation he decried. As he commented later, "I must confess that the duties of deportation were never very pleasant to me and often very bitter. Our deportation laws are inexorable and in many cases inhuman, particularly as they apply to men and women of honest behavior whose only crime is that they dared enter the promised land without conforming to law. I have seen hundreds of such persons forced back to the countries they came from, penniless, and at times without coats on their backs. I have seen families separated, never to be reunited."[19] The deportation increase also raised the problem of securing permission from former countries to accept the deported immigrant. Homeland nations did not always want their compatriots back and investigated the deportee's case thoroughly before deciding what to do. If denied, the individual had no legal homeland and could be indefinitely detained at Ellis or Angel Island.

As dictatorships emerged in Europe and persecution of minorities surged, particularly against Jews, a new demand for increased immigration occurred. Congress and the White House debated immigration policy in regard to refugees, but expressed little support for changing the restrictive laws set in the 1920s. With a still depressed economy and a general unwillingness to admit refugees who might compete for jobs, Congress refused to significantly open the doors to America. Furthermore, the anti-Semitism evident in the United States at that time, which Nazi propaganda and numerous local fascist groups encouraged, precluded a generous response to people fleeing concentration camps and violence. Roosevelt did not make significant efforts to reverse the immigration restrictions for refugees until 1938, and even by that late date, with violence against German Jews exploding, there were only half-hearted attempts. The U.S. State Department, which included some clearly anti-Semitic individuals, made it difficult for refugees to receive visas to enter the United States. Ellis Island and other immigration stations, including Angel Island, could have been put to good use as havens for innocent victims of bigotry. The immigration staff was available, the buildings remained in good shape (at Angel Island until 1940), with new ones unused, but the voice of the American people emphatically said "No." In effect, the nativists, restrictionists, and eugenicists had won.

Aftermath of Chinese Restrictions at Angel Island

Chinese immigrants remained concerned about exclusion even after entry. The government continued its effort to expel the Chinese, bolstered by the suspected number of paper sons. Although Europeans gaining entry at Ellis or Angel Island remained essentially on probation for three years, the Chinese stayed a suspect group for a much longer period and a target for government investigations and intimidation. Although Chinese Americans complained to government officials, the intensity of the attempt to deport remained strong. Even after Congress finally repealed the exclusion laws in 1943, during a time when China allied with the United States against Japan in World War II, anxiety remained strong among paper sons worrying that they would be revealed as illegal entries. Especially after 1949, when the Communists won the Chinese civil war, the investigations increased, and immigrants' fears raised during the immigration period never relented. Only after the Chinese Six Companies and the Immigration Service reached a compromise in 1956 with the "Confession Program," allowing those who had entered illegally to confess their actions and name other family members as part of the subterfuge, would these Chinese be allowed to apply for legal status. Many did not join this program out of continued concern about deportation, the cost of legal proceedings, and mistrust regarding the Immigration Service. Although the Chinese faced more discrimination than other Asians and more than Europeans, they created new lives across America in the same manner as other immigrants.

As the immigration laws and processing system changed, so did the need for these large immigration stations. Their value as entry points to America decreased after the quota laws, the overseas medical inspections, and the Great Depression.

Epilogue

ANGEL ISLAND CLOSED in 1940 following a devastating fire that destroyed the main building. In the midst of the fire, and as people evacuated the buildings, the guards maintained the station's racial and gender segregation practices. Women were placed in the hospital building, while the Chinese and European men each went to separate areas. A San Francisco building eventually became the processing center. The U.S. Army took control of the island station in 1941 and utilized it for army soldiers, captured German and Japanese military, and enemy aliens being moved inland. When World War II ended, Angel Island became the processing center for Japanese soldiers and others being sent back to Japan and for U.S. soldiers being released from service. The island stayed empty after that, and the remaining Angel Island buildings fell into disrepair. The California State Parks department had plans to demolish all buildings and create recreational space.

As the demolition went forward, Alexander Weiss, a park ranger, saw the Chinese writing still evident on the detention barrack walls in 1970 and realized that they constituted an important part of history. Once San Francisco's Asian American—and especially the Chinese American—community learned of these writings, they launched a campaign to preserve this historic site, and after much effort from this group and others, California agreed in 1976 to safeguard the barracks. A campaign to refurbish the station and create a museum then began. To the descendants of those who came through

Angel Island, the restoration engendered strong emotions. Connie Young Yu's grandmother was an Angel Island immigrant. Yu remarked that "the immigration barracks, with the expressions of suffering and struggle visible on the walls, is a fitting memorial to the courage and determination of our ancestors . . . It would serve as a reminder of America's past discriminatory policies toward Asians, and strengthen our resolve to continue to oppose any return of racial exclusion laws and detention centers." Furthermore, a refurbished station "meant restoring dignity, honor, and freedom to the pioneering immigrants."[1] Many Angel Island detainees had never spoken about their encounter with American immigration policies. Not only did the restoration reveal a forgotten or unknown part of America's multicultural past, but it opened up the history to many Angel Island detainees' progeny.

The public did not regard Angel Island in the same symbolic way they eventually considered Ellis Island. The Angel Island station had indicated clearly the racism in America's immigration laws, and Americans did not look upon it as a source of pride for American equality and justice. The Asian American community, through the Angel Island Immigration Station Historical Advisory Committee, however, made a significant effort to secure legislative support, to develop a cost estimate of the renovation, and to research the station's historical background. Historians, other scholars, and community leaders interviewed many former detainees, thereby providing the stories that would personalize the site. The Advisory Committee in a 1976 report stated what Angel Island represented to the Asian community and to U.S. history: "Angel Island Immigration Station presents the first, the only, and the best opportunity to fully interpret the history of Asian immigration to the United States. This is our Plymouth Rock, our Valley Forge, our Alamo, our Statue of Liberty, our Lincoln Memorial all rolled into one . . . In the same way that Ellis Island has been enshrined as a national monument to commemorate European immigration to America, Angel Island Immigration Station should be recognized and declared a National Historic Landmark."[2]

Based on the Advisory Committee's work, and with the support of the California legislature, the island station barracks were preserved and the effort to actually restore them began. Most importantly, the wall writings had to be safeguarded. The barracks and the exhibits opened in 1983, but more work needed to be done to fully restore the site and to make the American public aware of its importance in U.S. immigration history. The National Register of Historic Places recognized the station as a National Historic Landmark in

1997, and in 1999, the National Historic Trust for Historic Preservation considered Angel Island, as well as Ellis Island, two of the nation's most endangered historic sites. This designation spurred on the efforts at both islands to secure funds for full restoration. Given the public's enthusiasm for the Ellis Island immigration story, supporters wanted to bring the Angel Island history into the same context. The executive director of the Angel Island Immigration Station Foundation, Katherine Toy, said it best in her appearance before a congressional subcommittee in 2000: "Angel Island and Ellis Island serve as bookends to the national story of immigration, not only in geography, but also in meaning and experience. While Angel Island Immigration Station represents a difficult chapter in our national history, it is ultimately a story of triumph and of the perseverance of immigrants to endure and establish new lives in this country." As Lynn Woolsey, a California congresswoman, related, "Millions of Asian descendants nationwide are eager to see their roots in this country honored in the same way that we honor Ellis Island."[3] Congress awarded funds for full restoration in 2005. Although the project was not yet finished owing to budget issues, the official opening of the Angel Island immigration center occurred in February 2009.

Ellis Island facilities remained open until 1954, but the years of heavy use had already come to an end. During World War II, the island's buildings housed enemy aliens. The U.S. government arrested suspected Nazis who were German citizens but living in the United States, as well as their Italian and Japanese counterparts who favored their homeland regimes, and brought many to the island. This group remained small, numbering only a few hundred. The government released some individuals relatively quickly after review. Others stayed at Ellis Island for years, eventually being either sent back to their homelands or released. The new activity in relation to detainees made the island valuable again, but the traditional immigration services moved in 1943 to the former Works Progress Administration building in Manhattan.

Into the 1950s, the island remained a place to house suspected subversives of foreign citizenship with a Nazi, Fascist, or now Communist connection. The Internal Security Act of 1950, which called for the exclusion of alien Communist or Fascist Party members, led to the investigation and detention of those suspected of membership. The *New York Times Magazine* in 1950 reported that immigrants "believing until their arrival that they had passed the last barrier when they obtained visas and boat tickets . . . were baffled and bitterly disappointed" when taken to Ellis Island and detained for security checks.[4] On little evidence, new arrivals faced interrogation at Ellis Island. The Immigration and Naturalization Service also arrested and transferred to the island alleged undocumented aliens already residing in the New York area who might be subversives. The arrested aliens numbered about 1,500. The fear of allowing possible Communists into the United States remained strong during the 1950s McCarthy Red Scare period and led to inequities regarding immigrants held without proof of wrongdoing. Finally, after many complaints, revised laws allowed those arrivals to enter who had only titular membership in suspect organizations and who had involuntarily joined. People who had joined Communist or Fascist organizations as children, for example, no longer faced exclusion. Yet, the intention of the Internal Security Act is suggested by its namesake, Senator Patrick McCarran (R-NV), who claimed in 1951 that up to five million illegal aliens were in the United States and that they largely consisted of "militant Communists, Sicilian bandits and other criminals."[5] Combining the nativist, eugenicist, and anti-Italian attitudes of previous years with the Communist hysteria of the 1950s, McCarran managed to tie together two periods of ignorance and intolerance.

The Cold War detentions sullied America's reputation, as well as Ellis Island's symbolic role. Arresting people because of their supposed political views suggested a similarity in policy to America's Communist enemies. Furthermore, the island's facilities were lacking. Some areas, such as the hospital and the larger dining rooms, had been shut down already. The station at times became overcrowded, but government officials provided an infirmary and restarted a school for the detainees' children, indicating that those held at the station included not just detainees but their families as well. With a change in detention policy and no desire to maintain Ellis Island facilities anymore, as a result of its cost of almost a million dollars a year, the island station closed in November 1954.

In the immediate following years, the American public forgot about Ellis Island. The government even put the island up for sale amid suggestions that it could be utilized for such purposes as oil storages and warehouses, a resort, a park, or a drug rehabilitation facility. Nothing happened, however, and the land and buildings deteriorated. Many voices eventually began to be heard regarding the island's future: from Edward Corsi, from historians, and from those who entered the United States through Ellis Island, to preserve the place as a national monument to immigration and, as Corsi said in 1962, to "the welding together of many nationalities, races, and religions into a united nation, bound together by freedom and equality of opportunity," although clearly this was an overstatement.[6] By the 1960s, changes in attitudes toward the former immigrants were palpable. No longer regarded as the unwanted, "wretched refuse" of foreign lands but rather as part of America's greatness and strength, the public lauded these mainly European immigrants and their successive generations. Although this transformation did not signify the end of nativism, of attacking immigrants as bringing disease and decline to America, threatening American cultural values, and outbreeding better Americans, the alteration indicated a new stage for European immigrants. The Immigration Act of 1965, which ended the national origins quota system, is an illustration of the shift. No longer for sale, Ellis Island became, by executive order, part of the National Park system. But still, what to do with it?

After a number of false starts to restore the island's buildings and a short-lived public opening in 1976–1977, the National Park Service started to collect funds in 1981 to restore the island station and the Statue of Liberty, both to be completed by the 100th year of their initial openings. A public-private fundraising initiative, the Statue of Liberty–Ellis Island Foundation, led by Lee Iacocca, former head of Ford and Chrysler, raised most of the restoration money. With funds available from the foundation, the National Park Service moved ahead with plans to restore the main building and develop a museum. They refurbished the Great Hall reception building and made exhibits available as part of the Ellis Island Immigration Museum. Furthermore, Iacocca developed an Immigrant Wall of Honor, including the names of those who came through Ellis Island or immigrated at other ports. The public began visiting in 1990. Other buildings saw restoration after that date.

However, what the island should represent became a controversy. Should it be a monument to immigration's success or tell the real story of the Island of Hope, the Island of Tears? Many Americans equated Ellis Island with Plymouth Rock as the new starting point for America's people. This idea began to take hold given that a substantial number of Americans traced their ancestry to Ellis Island. Louis Adamic gave an earlier statement that illustrated the thinking about the two national symbols: "The beginning of their vital American background as groups is not the glorified Mayflower, but the as yet unglorified immigrant steerage; not Plymouth Rock or Jamestown, but Castle Garden or Ellis Island or Angel Island or the International Bridge or the Mexican and Canadian border, not the wilderness of New England, but the socio-economic jungle of the city slums and the factory system."[7] As a generation of Ellis Island Americans and their descendants began to achieve success and power within U.S. society, and looking back nostalgically at immigration and the island, they gave more attention to the concept of preservation as a national monument. Controversy over Ellis Island symbolism and what it says about who had value for America continued amid complaints about venerating certain newcomers to America and leaving out others who came not as immigrants, came before or after, or were already in America. While the Ellis Island museum adjusted to include other Americans, it is still most meaningful to those whose ancestors came through its doors.

What does Ellis Island's and Angel Island's history tell us about immigration to America? Processing at Ellis Island, while sometimes unfair and certainly anxiety producing for many worried about detention or exclusion, still worked relatively well. Inspectors and doctors examined, questioned, and processed millions through the station in its operational years. Most immigrants went through the station in a matter of a day or days. Ellis Island illustrated an enormous undertaking even with the corruption, the prejudice of inspectors and others, and the overcrowded sleeping and detention facilities evident. Efforts to have the processing run more smoothly could never satisfy everyone: restrictionists, ethnic communities, newspapers looking for stories, the American public divided on the immigration issue, and the immigrants themselves. Large-scale immigrant processing had never been done so quickly before and included so many arrivals. Ellis Island and even Angel Island reached a more efficient and superior level to what had existed before to handle immigration. The Ellis Island examination line was masterly in its expediency. A well-equipped hospital handled more patients with more unusual diseases from more countries than any other hospital in the United States.

Some serious problems remained throughout this early period of large-scale immigration. The steerage journey to Ellis and Angel Islands needed substantial improvement as a result of inadequate accommodations. The ship did not provide acceptable food and medical care. For those who spent all their funds to travel to a port city and pay for the transatlantic voyage, only to be rejected at the island stations, these occurrences represented a serious and sad flaw in the system. But a better system emerged in 1925 through an inspection process begun in overseas ports which American consulates handled.

However, Ellis Island represented much more than a processing station. The station embodies two streams of American thought. One was of acceptance, a civic nationalism that promised equality and fairness to all who came to the United States and stayed to live on its land regardless of race, religion, or nationality.[8] This approach welcomed diversity and saw in differences a strength that would enable the United States to be a beacon to the world. That beacon existed for the many who came during the high immigration years of the late nineteenth and early twentieth century, as for those who still come today. America symbolically represented the land of opportunity, a new beginning, even for those who came only to make money and return to their homeland, with Ellis Island as the main gateway.

But Ellis Island and especially Angel Island signified another aspect of American beliefs: racial nationalism. Many Americans considered the United States, a majority Protestant nation settled largely by northern Europeans, as an exclusionary nation that kept out the "wretched refuse" of Europe and elsewhere. As a result, strict immigration laws eventually barred those who appeared unable to add to America's racial, moral, and industrial strength. As various peoples passed through U.S. immigration gates, legislation and preference in law and sometimes in inspection provided an easier entry to those who looked like the original white settlers of this nation. Catholics, Jews, southern and eastern Europeans, Asians, and Africans often did not receive a welcoming reception as immigrants and faced a more difficult time being accepted into American society. Class distinctions existed as well. Those arriving in first- or second-class cabins rather than steerage obtained privileged treatment and when possible were kept separate from the "inferior" people.

These two ideological views shaped U.S. immigration policy and still play a role in contemporary America. They operated at the same time, offering contradictory policies. But other factors existed as well. The country's industrial needs at times conflicted with its racial/ethnic ideology, and a constant tug-of-war played out in the laws and inspections that determined who was allowed to enter and who could contribute to America's economy and unity. Progressive Era politics required that government use its powers to regulate and organize for the nation's betterment. Not only industries but also immigration came under close control. Ellis Island represents just one example of the demand to use federal power for society's good (as interpreted by some); Americanization, Prohibition, antitrust legislation, worker compensation laws, recall voting, and immigration restriction, to name a few, indicated the Progressive Era's push for regulation.

But ultimately the question was, Who would be a good American? Who would not disrupt the nation's democratic system and racial unity? The U.S. public sometimes listened to its nativist voices. During Ellis Island's high immigration years, nativist societies such as the American Protective Association, the Immigration Restriction League, and the Ku Klux Klan vowed to preserve an Anglo-Saxon America. Influential writers such as Madison Grant in *The Passing of the Great Race* (1916) spelled out the threat to American strength and "purity" of letting inferior, non-Nordic races enter and breed. Immigration restriction legislation of the 1920s put stricter exclusionary concepts into law and determined quotas for preferred and unwanted immigrants. Eugenicists added their "racial science" to the conversation. Few Americans wanted a complete end to immigration, but rather the entry of the "best" stock. Lesser races (nationalities) could be admitted, but only after careful medical inspection and guarantees that they would not become public charges, not destroy the government through radicalism, and not pollute the nation's racial stock. Most importantly, immigrants could not overwhelm the Anglo-Saxon majority. Nonwhites did not have an equal place in a European-based white America. The 1882 Chinese Exclusion Act and the differences between the treatment of European arrivals at Ellis and Angel Islands and that of Asians especially at Angel Island indicate clearly who the public most favored. The various immigration laws from 1882 to 1924 which increased the list of undesirable traits and the way inspectors interpreted these laws added further impediments to immigrant admission. Physical and mental conditions, public charge concerns, political beliefs, literacy, and even physique came into play during the arrivals' processing. Many Public Health doctors looked askance at southern and eastern Europeans, accepted stereotypes of these groups, and believed that English, German, and Scandinavian immigrants would make better Americans than Jews, Italians, and Poles.

Yet, even though restricted categories increased, the United States saw millions of immigrants enter during these early years, including thousands of Asians coming through Angel Island. The paradox of American immigration history and of the Ellis and Angel Island stories is that an acceptance of most immigrants for economic and at times humanitarian reasons won out over the naysayers who predicted doom for this country if restriction was not more forcefully imposed.

By the 1920s, however, racial nationalism prevailed, with the quota laws practically ending immigration from southern and eastern Europe. Asian immigration, having already faced severe restrictions, now experienced even more exclusionary legislation. Questions once again arose about racial purity, race preservation, and the failure of the melting pot. The earlier support for immigration from America's corporate leaders faded. World War I had cut off European immigration and required industry to find workers elsewhere, and they did in Mexico and the American South. With eugenicists maintaining a strong anti-immigration voice and hostility toward southern and eastern Europeans and Asians increasing, the pro-immigration forces were beaten. The 1930s Great Depression decreased immigration further, as did World War II. The high tide of immigration ended for that period.

Although these laws remained virtually in effect until 1965, immigrants still arrived through special laws for war brides, refugees, displaced persons, and those fleeing Communist governments. The repeal of the Chinese Exclusion Act in 1943 and the Immigration and Nationality Act of 1952 represents the first significant breaks with a restrictionist past. With the United States as a world power after World War II, and fighting a Cold War with the Soviet Union, immigration and the general treatment of minorities became international concerns. Although the 1952 act retained quotas, it did not exclude any race or nationality. Radical activities in the form of Communist proclivities led to exclusion similar to earlier legislation regarding radicalism, and small quotas from some countries such as China still existed. Nonetheless, change was occurring.

The 1965 Immigration Act renewed the immigration surge into the United States. However, as Congress developed this act, they designed the legislation to increase the number of European immigrants, particularly from Poland, Greece, and Italy. All Europeans, as they became part of a larger white population, achieved a welcome status not seen before. The 1965 act did remove country quotas and allowed immigration to be based on family reunification and skills desired in the United States. However, rather than the expected Europeans arriving, large numbers of Asian, African, Latin American, and Caribbean immigrants began making the journey. Immigration patterns changed, and nativist attitudes reappeared. While eugenics became discredited after the Holocaust's horror, a sense of who could be an acceptable immigrant and who could not be assimilated still existed.

Although immigrants no longer arrive by boats steaming into New York, San Francisco, or other ports, the controversy over acceptance continues in the same fashion as before. Will immigrants bring disease, un-American behaviors, and moral and economic decline to this land? Immigrants look different from those who came before, with the major sending countries no longer being Russia, Italy, or Poland, but instead Mexico, India, and China.

The immigration procedure in contemporary America resembles aspects of the earlier processing. As the twenty-first century began, potential immigrants desiring to enter the United States legally had to petition the U.S. Citizenship and Immigration Services (USCIS) for a visa (first required in 1924). A U.S. citizen, permanent resident, or employer must sponsor the petition. Immigrants who have their petition approved go to the American consulate or embassy for their document processing. The consular official determines whether the immigrants are eligible for the visa for which they are applying. Immigrants need a sponsor's affidavit of support in most cases, or an indication of adequate funds or a guaranteed job, along with a birth certificate, marriage/divorce certificates, and police records, and must have a medical exam and an interview. Once granted a visa, immigrants are free to travel to the United States within six months and begin the road to citizenship. A visa does not guarantee entry, and applicants can also be denied a visa based on familiar Ellis Island restrictions: likely to become a public charge, having a skill or seeking a job that competes with American workers or lowers their wages, having a communicable disease or other physical or mental disease that could pose a threat, polygamy, criminal record, fraudulent documents, and/or terrorist activity/espionage or other threats to the U.S. government, including immigrants belonging voluntarily to terrorist organizations. Ellis and Angel Islands and other immigrant stations are no longer functional, but restrictions are still operative and problems still exist, particularly in relation to concerns over terrorists and undocumented immigrants entering the country post–9/11.

As a result of terrorist fears, detention has become an issue again. Since 9/11, many Muslim men in the United States on student, tourist, and various temporary visas have been detained until they could be investigated. A large number have been deported. The whole visa processing system changed for Arab and Muslim men in an effort to provide more scrutiny before allowing entry into the United States. The handling of potential immigrants from certain countries became more like the process at Angel Island rather than Ellis Island. In effect, Muslim and Arab men were considered inadmissible until shown differently, much like the earlier Chinese immigrants. In terms of official government authority, and as a reflection of the new emphasis, the Department of Homeland Security became the agency overseeing immigration in 2003. The Immigration and Naturalization Service became three agencies under Homeland Security: USCIS manages legal immigration in regard to naturalization, immigrant benefits, petitions to bring relatives to the United States, and temporary work visas; Immigration and Customs Enforcement deals with investigations of all immigration matters, supervises over 250 detention centers throughout the United States, including those detainees in jails and privately operated prisons (although these have little government supervision), deports illegal and inadmissible immigrants, and controls further immigrant processing; and Customs and Border Protection handles illegal border incursions and, as with the other agencies, protects the United States from terrorists entering the country. National security is stressed in these agencies in a different way from earlier years of eugenic and health issues. Immigrant detentions have increased from about 70,000 in 1998 to 400,000 in 2013. Detention facilities, as in the Ellis and Angel Island days, are often criticized for poor care, mistreatment of immigrants, and, particularly similar to Angel Island, long detentions of months or years. Pedro Guzman, detained at the Stewart Detention Center in Georgia, echoed the sentiment of Angel Island poems: "After twenty months away from home, you lose faith, you feel worthless . . . This place breaks you. The constant screaming and verbal abuse by the guards is just made to break your soul and handicap you."[9]

For later immigrants, reasons for emigration remained primarily the same: religious freedom, opportunity, escape from war, poverty, and especially the possibility to start a new life. But differences exist. Stella Dushats, a Jewish immigrant from the Soviet Union arriving in 1977 at age 40, illustrates what it was like for Europeans coming to America after the Ellis Island period. Not poverty stricken and already having a career in her former country, she flew to the United States and, in one important similarity to the past, found help from the Hebrew Immigrant Aid Society. Social service agencies remained crucial in the adjustment process, particularly in finding the immigrants employment and places to live. As she says, "It wasn't the same process as the people who came through Ellis Island. This was organized before we left—an organized immigration process. We had a visa just to get here, and then as soon as we came, HIAS has wonderful volunteers here . . . And they took care of us."[10] As earlier, immigrants had to learn English, although not all did, and as before, when they visited their relatives in their former country, they tried to convince them to emigrate. With a different immigration experience, Jorge Munoz from Colombia crossed the border from Mexico to California in 1980 at age 16. He and his family arrived in Mexico by plane and then crossed the border illegally and later went to New York. As he said, "We were just immigrants looking for freedom." Munoz eventually was allowed to become a citizen as a result of laws passed which gave undocumented immigrants the right to move on to citizenship. Munoz worked hard, saved some money, devoted himself to helping other immigrants, and started a new life. His attitude toward America is not unlike those who came earlier: "I don't think I would ever move back to Colombia . . . I've established my life here . . . You know, people think that we are a problem—the immigrants. We are not a problem!"[11]

Images of America did not change from earlier times. Tunde Ayobami, coming from Nigeria in 1969, speaks of hearing good things about America and yearning to come to the United States. But reality set in when he emigrated. "I was disappointed for the fact that money wasn't easy to get. Judging from the Hollywood pictures and how people were smashing cars and everybody walk leisurely on the street, I thought I was going to a paradise; you don't have to earn money."[12]

America's love-hate relationship with immigration continues, and race and religion still play a role. White Cubans received more favorable acceptance than Black Haitians when those arriving from these countries sought to enter. After 9/11 Muslims were regarded as suspect and treated in a similar way as earlier immigrants thought to be anarchists or Communists. A "Red Ark" like the one that sent back hundreds of suspected anarchists and revolutionaries to Russia in 1919 might find support in relation to suspected Muslim terrorists today. Although eugenics is largely forgotten, fear of immigrants for various other reasons remains.

Illegal or undocumented immigrants are a major concern in contemporary America. Prior to the 1880s and the Page Act, states inefficiently restricted immigration. Undocumented aliens were not evident since few laws existed. Into the Ellis Island years, rejection rates hovered at about 2 percent of new arrivals at the island, but many more faced detention. Even with inspections, the great majority of detainees, as well as some undocumented immigrants, came into the country. At Angel Island, through the "paper sons" technique, more illegal immigrants secured admittance. Racial/ethnic aspects of this concern are still apparent. Undocumented immigrants crossing the U.S.-

Mexico border are a constant subject of legislative and public anxiety. Yet, if hundreds of thousands of Germans, English, or Norwegians arrived illegally, the concern would be much less. In fact, Congress passed special laws in the 1980s to allow more Irish into the United States.

The division in American attitudes toward immigrants remains in contemporary times. How America will respond to the absorption of these immigrants is still a major question.

NOTES

CHAPTER ONE: How (and Why) Immigrants Traveled to America

1. John Lukasavicius and Mary Strokonos quoted in Bruce Stave and John F. Sutherland with Aldo Salerno, *From the Old Country: An Oral History of European Migration to America* (New York: Twayne, 1994), 28, 36, unnamed Lithanian immigrant quoted on p. 17; Bartunek quoted in David M. Brownstone, Irene M. Franck, and Douglass L. Brownstone, *Island of Hope, Island of Tears* (New York; Rawson, Wade, 1979), 49–50; Fino quoted in Michael La Sorte, *La Merica: Images of Italian Greenhorn Experience* (Philadelphia: Temple University Press, 1985), 7; Victor Tartarini, interviewed by Debby Dane, Nov. 22, 1985, Interview Number 094, Ellis Island Oral History Project, United States Department of the Interior, National Park Service; Sadie Carilli, interviewed by Dana Gumb, Oct. 11, 1985, Interview Number 047, Ellis Island Oral History Project; Julia Goniprow quoted in Joan Morrison and Charlotte Fox Zabusky, *American Mosaic: The Immigrant Experience in the Words of Those Who Lived It* (Pittsburgh: University of Pittsburgh Press, 1980), 68; Covello quoted in Dale R. Steiner, *Of Thee I Sing: Immigrants and American History* (New York: Harcourt Brace Jovanovich, 1987), 179.

2. Quoted in Irving Howe, *World of Our Fathers* (New York: Harcourt Brace Jovanovich, 1976), 60.

3. Quoted in John B. Weber, *Autobiography of John B. Weber* (Buffalo, NY: J. W. Clement, 1924), 127–128, 124.

4. Quoted in Vincent J. Cannato, *American Passage: The History of Ellis Island* (New York: HarperCollins, 2009), 67.

5. Jeong quoted in Emmy E. Werner, *Passages to America: Oral Histories of Child Immigrants from Ellis Island and Angel Island* (Washington, DC: Potomac Books, 2009), 136; other immigrants quoted in Erika Lee and Judy Yung, *Angel Island: Immigrant Gateway to America* (New York: Oxford University Press, 2010), 71; and Him Mark Lai, Genny Lim, and Judy Yung, *Island: Poetry and History of Chinese Immigrants on Angel Island, 1910–1940* (Seattle: University of Washington Press, 1980), 48.

6. Quoted in Brownstone, Franck, and Brownstone, *Island of Hope*, 53, see also 17.

7. Quoted in Howe, *World of Our Fathers*, 36; quoted in Sydney Stahl Weinberg, *The World of Our Mothers: The Lives of Jewish Immigrant Women* (Chapel Hill: University of North Carolina Press, 1988), 77–79.

8. Peter Morton Coan, *Ellis Island Interviews: Immigrants Tell Their Stories in Their Own Words* (New York: Barnes and Noble, 1997), 39.

9. Information of immigration restriction laws can be found in Roger Daniels, *Guarding the Golden Door: American Immigration Policy and Immigrants since 1882* (New York: Hill and Wang, 2004); Alan M. Kraut, *The Huddled Masses: The Immigrant in American Society, 1880–1921* (Arlington Heights, IL: Harlan Davidson, 1982); Barry Moreno, *Encyclopedia of Ellis Island* (Westport, CT: Greenwood Press, 2004).

10. Amy L. Fairchild, *Science at the Borders: Immigrant Medical Inspection and the Shaping of the Modern Industrial Labor Force* (Baltimore: Johns Hopkins University Press, 2003).

11. Cannato, *American Passage*, 161–162.

12. Quoted in Thomas M. Pitkin, *Keepers of the Gate: A History of Ellis Island* (New York: New York University Press, 1975), 43.

13. Cannato, *American Passage*, 404.

14. Quoted in Fitzhugh Mullan, *Plagues and Politics: The Story of the United States Public Health Service* (New York: Basic Books, 1989), 41.

15. Cannato, *American Passage*, 222; Douglas C. Baynton, "Defectives in the Land: Disability and American Immigration Policy, 1882–1924," *Journal of American Ethnic History* 24, no. 3 (Spring 2005): 41.

16. Mary Antin, *The Promised Land* (Boston: Houghton Mifflin, 1912), 175, 177.

17. Quoted in Moreno, *Encyclopedia of Ellis Island*, 90–91.

18. Quoted in Weinberg, *World of Our Mothers*, 79.

19. Quoted in Coan, *Ellis Island Interviews*, 42.

20. Allan McLaughlin, "How Immigrants Are Inspected," *Popular Science Monthly* 66 (1905): 357.

21. La Sorte, *La Merica*, 16.

22. Robert Eric Barde, *Immigration at the Golden Gate: Passenger Ships, Exclusion, and Angel Island* (Westport, CT: Praeger, 2008), 109.

23. Quoted in Howe, *World of Our Fathers*, 41–42.

24. Coan, *Ellis Island Interviews*, 45.

25. Edward A. Steiner, *On the Trail of the Immigrant* (New York: Fleming H. Revell, 1906), 36; on meat served, see Moreno, *Encyclopedia of Ellis Island*, 228.

26. Quoted in Coan, *Ellis Island Interviews*, 54.

27. Quoted in Brownstone, Franck, and Brownstone, *Island of Hope*, 121–122; Strokonos quoted in Stave and Sutherland with Salerno, *From the Old Country*, 29.

28. Quoted in Duffy oral history, excerpts Ellis Island Oral History Collection; Chinese immigrants quoted in Lee and Yung, *Angel Island*, 73.

29. Annual Report of the Commissioner-General of Immigration quoted in Halan D. Unrau, *The Historic Resource Study: Ellis Island–Statue of Liberty National Monument*, vol. 2 (Washington, DC: National Park Service, 1984), 601.

30. Quoted in Moses Rischin, *The Promised City: New York's Jews, 1870–1914* (New York: Corinth Books, 1964), 33.

31. Quoted in Brownstone, Franck, and Brownstone, *Island of Hope*, 133.

32. La Sorte, *La Merica*, 29–30.

33. Broughton Brandenburg, *Imported Americans: The Story of the Experiences of a Disguised American and His Wife Studying the Immigration Question* (New York: Frederick A. Stokes, 1904), 200.

34. Quoted in Brownstone, Franck, and Brownstone, *Island of Hope*, 103.

35. Ibid., 145.

36. Quoted in Coan, *Ellis Island Interviews*, 49; Louis Adamic, *Laughing in the Jungle: The Autobiography of an Immigrant in America* (New York: Harper and Brothers, 1932), 40.

37. Quoted in Werner, *Passages to America*, 26–29.

38. Edward Corsi, *In the Shadow of Liberty: The Chronicle of Ellis Island* (New York: MacMillan, 1935), 3–4.

39. Manny Steen, interviewed by Paul Sigrist, Mar. 22, 1991, excerpts from Ellis Island Oral History Collection.

40. Quoted in La Sorte, *La Merica*, 40.

41. Cannato, *American Passage*, 53.

42. Quoted in Him Mark Lai, "Island of Immortals: Chinese Immigrants and the Angel Island Immigration Station," *California History* 57, no. 1 (1978): 90–91; quoted in Barde, *Immigration at the Golden Gate*, 70.

43. Quoted in Brownstone, Franck, and Brownstone, *Island of Hope*, 154.

44. Pitkin, *Keepers of the Gate*, 95.

45. Mrozowski quoted in Stave and Sutherland with Salerno, *From the Old Country*, 27; steamship official quoted in Cannato, *American Passage*, 299.

46. Quoted in Howard Markel, *Quarantine! East European Jewish Immigrants and the New York City Epidemics of 1892* (Baltimore: Johns Hopkins University Press, 1997), 25, 61–62, number of deaths on p. 67.

47. Quoted in Coan, *Ellis Island Interviews*, 49.

48. Brandenburg, *Imported Americans*, 208.

49. Corsi, *In the Shadow of Liberty*, 5.

50. Quoted in Brownstone, Franck, and Brownstone, *Island of Hope*, 155, 157.

51. Brandenburg, *Imported Americans*, 213.

52. Quoted in Barde, *Immigration at the Golden Gate*, 132–133.

53. Quoted in Pitkin, *Keepers of the Gate*, 21.

54. Ibid., 32.

55. Cannato, *American Passage*, 121.

56. Moreno, *Encyclopedia of Ellis Island*, 208.

57. Ibid., 27, 83–85, 106–107, 133, 139–140, 149–151.

58. Quoted in Pitkin, *Keepers of the Gate*, 32–33.

59. *San Francisco Chronicle* quoted in Barde, *Immigration at the Golden Gate*, 15–16; Husband quoted in Lai, "Island of Immortals," 93.

60. Quoted in Lee and Yung, *Angel Island*, 69; Lai, "Island of Immortals," 88–89; Lai, Lim, and Yung, *Island*, 12.

61. Quoted in Lee and Yung, *Angel Island*, 84–85.

62. Victor Safford, *Immigration Problems: Personal Experiences of an Official* (New York: Dodd, Mead, 1925), 35. Safford worked at Ellis Island from 1895 to 1905 as a medical officer, hospital administrator, examiner of mental cases, and early advocate of the line inspection system.

63. Quoted in Alfred C. Reed, "Going Through Ellis Island," *Popular Science Monthly*, Jan. 1913, 5–6.

64. E. Steiner, *On the Trail*, 72.

CHAPTER TWO: How Immigrants Were Processed

1. Thomas M. Pitkin, *Keepers of the Gate: A History of Ellis Island* (New York: New York University Press, 1975), 73; Harlan D. Unrau, *The Historic Resource Study: Ellis Island–Statue of Liberty National Monument*, vol. 1 (Washington, DC: National Park Service, 1984), 202.

2. Barry Moreno, *Encyclopedia of Ellis Island* (Westport, CT: Greenwood Press, 2004), 78.

3. See Erika Lee and Judy Yung, *Angel Island: Immigrant Gateway to America* (New York: Oxford University Press, 2010), 69; Robert Eric Barde, *Immigration at the Golden Gate: Passenger Ships, Exclusion, and Angel Island* (Westport, CT: Praeger, 2008), 18.

4. Louis Adamic, *Laughing in the Jungle: The Autobiography of an Immigrant in America* (New York: Harper and Brothers, 1932), 41; quoted in Unrau, *Historic Resource Study*, 3:1111.

5. Quoted in Peter Morton Coan, *Ellis Island Interviews: Immigrants Tell Their Stories in Their Own Words* (New York: Barnes and Noble, 1997), 284.

6. Edward A. Steiner, *On the Trail of the Immigrant* (New York: Fleming H. Revell, 1906), 65.

7. Quoted in David M. Brownstone, Irene M. Franck, and Douglass L. Brownstone, *Island of Hope, Island of Tears* (New York: Rawson, Wade, 1979), 177; Geddes quoted in Sir Auckland Geddes, *Despatch from H.M. Ambassador at Washington Reporting on Conditions at Ellis Island Immigration Station* (London: His Majesty's Stationery Office, 1923), 6.

8. Quoted in Edward Corsi, *In the Shadow of Liberty: The Chronicle of Ellis Island* (New York: MacMillan, 1935), 73, 76–77.

9. Quoted in Coan, *Ellis Island Interviews*, 124.

10. Quoted in Brownstone, Franck, and Brownstone, *Island of Hope*, 205, see also 216; Moreno, *Encyclopedia of Ellis Island*, 126.

11. Victor Safford, *Immigration Problems: Personal Experiences of an Official* (New York: Dodd, Mead), 248–249; Reed quoted in Moreno, *Encyclopedia of Ellis Island*, 142–143, see also 144, 163.

12. Mullan quoted in Moreno, *Encyclopedia of Ellis Island*, 144; Knight quoted in Vincent J. Cannato, *American Passage: The History of Ellis Island* (New York: HarperCollins, 2009), 252, see also 253.

13. Quoted in Cannato, *American Passage*, 253.

14. Quoted in Moreno, *Encyclopedia of Ellis Island*, 144.

15. Beatrice Cohen Conan, interviewed by Paul E. Sigrist Jr., July 25, 1995, Interview Number EI 646, Ellis Island Oral History Project, U.S. Department of the Interior, National Park Service.

16. Quoted in Lorie Conway, *Forgotten Ellis Island: The Extraordinary Story of America's Immigrant Hospital* (New York: HarperCollins, 2007), 59.

17. Quoted in Fiorello H. La Guardia, *The Making of an Insurgent, an Autobiography: 1882–1919* (New York: Capricorn Books, [1948] 1961), 64.

18. Broughton Brandenburg, *Imported Americans: The Story of the Experiences of a Disguised American and His Wife Studying the Immigration Question* (New York: Frederick A. Stokes, 1904), 201.

19. Quoted in Irving Howe, *World of Our Fathers* (New York: Harcourt Brace Jovanovich, 1976), 44; Roosevelt quote in Conway, *Forgotten Ellis Island*, 39.

20. Seymour Rexsite, interviewed by Debra Allee, Sept. 10, 1985, Interview Number 025, Ellis Island Oral History Project, U.S. Department of the Interior, National Park Service.

21. Steen quoted in Coan, *Ellis Island Interviews*, 124; Amy L. Fairchild, *Science at the Borders: Immigrant Medical Inspection and the Shaping of the Modern Industrial Labor Force* (Baltimore: Johns Hopkins University Press, 2003), 64.

22. Quoted in Brownstone, Franck, and Brownstone, *Island of Hope*, 208.

23. Quoted in Fairchild, *Science at the Borders*, 64.

24. Quoted in Conway, *Forgotten Ellis Island*, 20.

25. Quoted in Unrau, *Historic Resource Study*, 3:1113.

26. Moreno, *Encyclopedia of Ellis Island*, 42.

27. Quoted in Corsi, *In the Shadow of Liberty*, 76.

28. Quoted in Pitkin, *Keepers of the Gate*, 134.

29. Moreno, *Encyclopedia of Ellis Island*, 109, 123.

30. Fairchild, *Science at the Borders*, 32–37.

31. Quoted in Cannato, *American Passage*, 255.

32. Quoted in Philip Cowen, *Memories of an American Jew* (New York: International Press, 1932), 174–175; see also Bertha May Boody, *A Psychological Study of Immigrant Children at Ellis Island*, Mental Measurement Monographs Serial 3 (Baltimore: Williams and Wilkins, 1926), 100.

33. Quoted in John T. E. Richardson, "Howard Andrew Knox and the Origins of Performance Testing on Ellis Island, 1912–1916," *History of Psychology* 6, no. 2 (2003): 151, see also 152, 154; Boody, *Psychological Study*, 54–57.

34. Quoted in Richardson, "Howard Andrew Knox," 149, 158.

35. Cannato, *American Passage*, 247.

36. Alfred C. Reed, "Going Through Ellis Island," *Popular Science Monthly* 82 (January 1913): 7–8.

37. Quoted in Cannato, *American Passage*, 214; quoted in Conway, *Forgotten Ellis Island*, 125.

38. Fairchild, *Science at the Borders*, 103–104.

39. Alan M. Kraut, *Silent Travelers: Germs, Genes, and the "Immigrant Menace"* (Baltimore: Johns Hopkins University Press, 1994), 73–76; Cowen, *Memories of an American Jew*, 174.

40. Quoted in La Guardia, *Making of an Insurgent*, 65–66; quoted in Conway, *Forgotten Ellis Island*, 129.

41. Douglas C. Baynton, "Defective in the Land: Disability and American Immigration Policy, 1882–1924," *Journal of American Ethnic History* 24, no. 3 (Spring 2005): 35–37, quote on p. 36; Conway, *Forgotten Ellis Island*, 37–38; Konig case quoted in Cannato, *American Passage*, 208, Stallone on pp. 209–210.

42. Quoted in Cannato, *American Passage*, 210–211.

43. Quoted in Fairchild, *Science at the Borders*, 166, 168.

44. Cannato, *American Passage*, 212–221.

45. Quoted in ibid., 273, see also 266.

46. Quoted in ibid., 274.

47. Quoted in ibid., 303.

48. Quoted in Unrau, *Historic Resource Study*, 2:595, 548–549.

49. Adamic, *Laughing in the Jungle*, 44–45.

50. Quoted in Fairchild, *Science at the Borders*, 74.

51. Pitkin, *Keepers of the Gate*, 42; Nagel quoted in Cannato, *American Passage*, 223.

52. Cowen, *Memories of an American Jew*, 145–146.

53. Quoted in Lee and Yung, *Angel Island*, 227–228.

54. Fairchild, *Science at the Borders*, 134–139; poem and comment quoted in Him Mark Lai, Genny Lim, and Judy Yung, *Island: Poetry and History of Chinese Immigrants on Angel Island, 1910–1940* (Seattle: University of Washington Press, 1980), 100, 108.

55. Quoted in Lee and Yung, *Angel Island*, 46, 88.

56. Quoted in Erika Lee, *At America's Gates: Chinese Immigration during the Exclusion Era, 1882–1943* (Chapel Hill: University of North Carolina Press, 2003), 95–96.

57. Nagel quoted in ibid., 86; Leung quoted in Lai, Lim, and Yung, *Island*, 116; newspaper and commissioner-general quoted in Lee, *At America's Gates*, 84, 207.

58. Quoted in Lee, *At America's Gates*, 197.

59. James Louie and Albert Kai Wong quoted in Emmy E. Werner, *Passages to America: Oral Histories of Child Immigrants from Ellis Island and Angel Island* (Washington, DC: Potomac Books, 2009), 130–132.

60. Quoted in Lai, Lim, and Yung, *Island*, 114.

61. Lee and Yung, *Angel Island*, 93–94.

62. Corsi, *In the Shadow of Liberty*, 159.

63. Quoted in Lee, *At America's Gates*, 223.

64. Quoted in Unrau, *Historic Resource Study*, 2:254.

65. Quoted in Isaac Metzker, ed., *A Bintel Brief: Sixty Years of Letters from the Lower East Side to the Jewish Daily Forward* (New York: Doubleday, 1971), 99.

66. Aaron Chaifetz, interviewed by Debra Allee, Jan. 24, 1985, Interview Number 007; Charles T. Anderson, interviewed by Dana Gumb, Jan. 23, 1985, Interview

Number 005, Ellis Island Oral History Project, United States Department of the Interior, National Park Service.

67. Marie Jastrow, *A Time to Remember: Growing Up in New York before the Great War* (New York: W. W. Norton, 1979), 44–45.

68. Quoted in Corsi, *In the Shadow of Liberty*, 80.

69. Brandenburg, *Imported Americans*, 220.

70. Reed, "Going Through Ellis Island," 14.

71. Quoted in Coan, *Ellis Island Interviews*, 258.

72. Quoted in Werner, *Passages to America*, 27.

73. Weiss quoted in Brownstone, Franck, and Brownstone, *Island of Hope*, 207; Kevar quoted in Coan, *Ellis Island Interviews*, 248; Rose S. quoted in Sydney Stahl Weinberg, *The World of Our Mothers: The Lives of Jewish Immigrant Women* (Chapel Hill: University of North Carolina Press, 1988), 89.

74. Quoted in Unrau, *Historic Resource Study*, 3:1113.

CHAPTER THREE: How Newcomers Dealt with Delays and Coped with Detainment or Rejection

1. Michael La Sorte, *La Merica: Images of Italian Greenhorn Experience* (Philadelphia: Temple University Press, 1985), 31–32, 36.

2. Quoted in Harlan D. Unrau, *The Historic Resource Study: Ellis Island–Statue of Liberty National Monument*, vol. 3 (Washington, DC: National Park Service, 1984), 1098.

3. "Thirty Orphans Arrive, Bereaved by Massacres," *New York Times*, Magazine Section, Aug. 26, 1906.

4. Quoted in Bertha May Boody, *A Psychological Study of Immigrant Children at Ellis Island*, Mental Measurement Monographs Serial 3 (Baltimore: Williams and Wilkins, 1926), 105, see also 103–105; Barry Moreno, *Encyclopedia of Ellis Island* (Westport, CT: Greenwood Press, 2004), 216–218; Angela Maria Pirrone (Weinkam), interviewed by Nancy Dallett, Feb. 4, 1986, Interview Number 132, Ellis Island Oral History Project, U.S. Department of the Interior, National Park Service; Frederic C. Howe, *The Confessions of a Reformer* (New York: Charles Scribner's Sons, 1925), 256–257.

5. Annual Report of the Surgeon General of the Public Health Service, 1921, quoted in Unrau, *Historic Resource Study*, 2:632.

6. Quoted in Edward Corsi, *In the Shadow of Liberty: The Chronicle of Ellis Island* (New York: MacMillan, 1935), 73, 77–79; quoted in Thomas M. Pitkin, *Keepers of the Gate: A History of Ellis Island* (New York: New York University Press, 1975), 108.

7. Quoted in Lorie Conway, *Forgotten Ellis Island: The Extraordinary Story of America's Immigrant Hospital* (New York: HarperCollins, 2007), 61.

8. Quoted in Corsi, *In the Shadow of Liberty*, 78–79; David M. Brownstone, Irene M. Franck, and Douglas L. Brownstone, *Island of Hope, Island of Tears* (New York: Rawson, Wade, 1979), 183–184.

9. Henry H. Curran, *Pillar to Post* (New York: Charles Scribner's Sons, 1941), 291–292.

10. Quoted in Erika Lee and Judy Yung, *Angel Island: Immigrant Gateway to America* (New York: Oxford University Press, 2010), 96.

11. Quoted in Pitkin, *Keepers of the Gate*, 198; *Forward* letter quoted in Isaac Metzker, *A Bintel Brief: Sixty Years of Letters from the Lower East Side to the Jewish Daily Forward* (New York: Doubleday and Company, 1971), 99; Dobbin quoted in August C. Bolino, *The Ellis Island Source Book*, 2nd ed. (Washington, DC: Kensington Historical Press, 1990), 113.

12. Quoted in Pitkin, *Keepers of the Gate*, 108; "Reforms Effected at Ellis Island, 1920–21," quoted in Unrau, *Historic Resource Study*, 2:554.

13. Quoted in Curran, *From Pillar to Post*, 291, 293–294, 297.

14. Howe, McNeill, and Geddes quoted in Vincent J. Cannato, *American Passage: The History of Ellis Island* (New York: HarperCollins, 2009), 339–341; and last Geddes quote in Pitkin, *Keepers of the Gate*, 147–148.

15. Quoted in Unrau, *Historic Resource Study*, 3:909–910.

16. Lee and Yung, *Angel Island*, 56–63.

17. Quoted in Erika Lee, *At America's Gates: Chinese Immigration during the Exclusion Era, 1882–1943* (Chapel Hill: University of North Carolina Press, 2003), 128.

18. Him Mark Lai, "Island of Immortals: Chinese Immigrants and the Angel Island Immigration Station," *California History* 57, no. 1 (1978): 95.

19. Quoted in Robert Eric Barde, *Immigration at the Golden Gate: Passenger Ships, Exclusion, and Angel Island* (Westport, CT: Praeger, 2008), 18.

20. Quoted in Him Mark Lai, Genny Lin, and Judy Yung, *Island: Poetry and History of Chinese Immigrants on Angel Island, 1910–1940* (Seattle: University of Washington Press, 1980), 68.

21. Quoted in Lee and Yung, *Angel Island*, 99–100.

22. Quoted in ibid., 120.

23. Mark Wischnitzer, *Visas to Freedom: The History of HIAS* (Cleveland: World, 1956), 54, 64–67; Philip Cowen, *Memories of an American Jew* (New York: International Press, 1932), 169; La Sorte, *La Merica*, 60; Riegelman quote from Peter Morton Coan, *Ellis Island Interviews: Immigrants Tell Their Stories in Their Own Words* (New York: Barnes and Noble, 1997), 243; Barth quote from Brownstone, Franck, and Brownstone, *Island of Hope*, 230–231.

24. Cowen, *Memories of an American Jew*, 67; quote from Pitkin, *Keepers of the Gate*, 79–80.

25. Corsi, *In the Shadow of Liberty*, 101–103.

26. Pitkin, *Keepers of the Gate*, 77; Italian immigrant quoted in Bolino, *Ellis Island Source Book*, 114.

27. "Rebuttal of Commissioner Williams to Congressional Charges, April 1911," in Unrau, *Historic Resource Study*, 2:419.

28. Angela Carlozzi Rossi, interviewed by Margo Nash, Nov. 7, 1973, Interview Number NPS 28, Ellis Island Oral History Project.

29. Cowen, *Memories of an American Jew*, 152, 165; quoted in Emmy E. Werner, *Passages to America: Oral Histories of Child Immigrants from Ellis Island and Angel Island* (Washington, DC: Potomac Books, 2009), 22.

30. Conway, *Forgotten Ellis Island*, 135; Safford quote in Victor Safford, *Immigration Problems: Personal Experiences of an Official* (New York: Dodd, Mead, 1925), 52.

31. Quoted in Conway, *Forgotten Ellis Island*, 13, 8.

32. Assistant Surgeon, P.H.A to Commissioner of Immigration, July 16,1906, Box 8, Folder 116, Harlan D. Unrau Papers, Ellis Island Archives.

33. Josephine Friedman Lutomski, interviewed by Edward Applebome, Feb. 10, 1986, Interview Number AKRF 162, Ellis Island Oral History Project.

34. Quoted in Conway, *Forgotten Ellis Island*, 73–74.

35. Quoted in Unrau, *Historic Resource Study*, 2:634–635.

36. Lutomski, interviewed by Edward Applebome, Feb. 10, 1986.

37. Quoted in Conway, *Forgotten Ellis Island*, 17, 74, 75–76; Alfred C. Reed, "Going Through Ellis Island," *Popular Science Monthly* 82 (January 1913): 6; Anthony Merital, interviewed by Paul Sigrist, Sept. 26, 1991, Interview Number EI–98, Ellis Island Oral History Project, U.S. Department of the Interior, National Park Service; Dr. Morris Moel, interviewed by Nancy Dallett, Feb. 4, 1986, Interview Number 133, Ellis Island Oral History Project, U.S. Department of the Interior, National Park Service; Gorda story in "Grieving Mother Commits Suicide," *New York Times*, May 19, 1907.

38. Quoted in Conway, *Forgotten Ellis Island*, 41.

39. Ibid., 11.

40. "Ellis Island Jam Halts Immigration," *New York Times*, Sept. 24, 1920.

41. Quoted in Conway, *Forgotten Ellis Island*, 109.

CHAPTER FOUR: How the Immigration Staff and Others Viewed Their Work

1. Quoted in Thomas M. Pitkin, *Keepers of the Gate: A History of Ellis Island* (New York: New York University Press, 1975), 65.

2. Robert Eric Barde, *Immigration at the Golden Gate: Passenger Ships, Exclusion, and Angel Island* (Westport, CT: Praeger, 2008), 205; Erika Lee and Judy Yung, *Angel Island: Immigrant Gateway to America* (New York: Oxford University Press, 2010), 39.

3. Quoted in Lorie Conway, *Forgotten Ellis Island: The Extraordinary Story of America's Immigrant Hospital* (New York: HarperCollins, 2007), 38.

4. Dr. T. Bruce H. Anderson, interviewed by Elizabeth Yew, Sept. 22, 1977, Interview Number NPS 104; Dr. Robert L. Leslie, interviewed by Dana Gumb, Aug. 14, 1985, Interview Number AKRF 17; Leslie, interviewed by Guggenheim Productions, Oct. 22, 1985, Interview Number GPI 12; Dr. Grover A. Kemph, interviewed by Elizabeth Yew, Sept. 10–11, 1977, Interview Number NPS 101, Ellis Island Oral History Project, U.S. Department of the Interior, National Park Service.

5. Jacob Auerbach, interviewed by Janet Levine, Oct. 14, 1992, Interview Number EI 225; Sadie Guttman Kaplan, interviewed by Paul Sigrist, July 2, 1992, Interview Number EI 188, Ellis Island Oral History Project.

6. Broughton Brandenburg, *Imported Americans: The Story of the Experiences of a Disguised American and His Wife Studying the Immigration Question* (New York: Frederick A. Stokes, 1904), 214.

7. Him Mark Lai, Genny Lim, and Judy Yung, *Island: Poetry and History of Chinese Immigrants on Angel Island, 1910–1940* (Seattle: University of Washington Press, 1980), 108–109; quoted in Barde, *Immigration at the Golden Gate*, 250, 254–255; Lee and Yung, *Angel Island*, 42.

8. John B. Weber, *Autobiography of John B. Weber* (Buffalo, NY: J. W. Clement, 1924), 89–93. Weber was the first commissioner of immigration for Ellis Island.

9. Quoted in Barry Moreno, *Encyclopedia of Ellis Island* (Westport, CT: Greenwood Press, 2004), 174–175, 47.

10. Quoted in Edward Corsi, *In the Shadow of Liberty: The Chronicle of Ellis Island* (New York: MacMillan, 1935), 72–73, 76–77, 83.

11. Quoted in ibid., 264.

12. Powderly quoted in Harlan D. Unrau, *The Historic Resource Study: Ellis Island–Statue of Liberty National Monument*, vol. 2 (Washington, DC: National Park Service, 1984), 216, see also note on p. 217; quoted in Conway, *Forgotten Ellis Island*, 6.

13. "Many Want to Feed the Immigrants," *New York Times*, May 11, 1908.

14. Quoted in Corsi, *In the Shadow of Liberty*, 293.

15. Frederic C. Howe, *The Confessions of a Reformer* (New York: Charles Scribner's Sons, 1925), 259–262, quote on p. 262.

16. "Ellis Island Privileges," *New York Times*, June 21, 1902; Edward Corsi, *In the Shadow of Liberty*, 91.

17. Quoted in David M. Brownstone, Irene M. Franck, and Douglass L. Brownstone, *Island of Hope, Island of Tears* (New York: Rawson, Wade, 1979), 185.

18. Weber, *Autobiography*, 88.

19. Quoted in Pitkin, *Keepers of the Gate*, 89.

20. Quoted in Moreno, *Encyclopedia of Ellis Island*, 47.

21. Lai, Lim, and Yung, *Island*, 115; letter quoted in Barde, *Immigration at the Golden Gate*, 211.

22. Quoted in Barde, *Immigration at the Golden Gate*, 226–227.

23. Ibid., 227.

24. Ibid., 249–250.

25. Conway, *Forgotten Ellis Island*, 153; Victor Safford, *Immigration Problems: Personal Experiences of an Official* (New York: Dodd, Mead, 1925), 228.

26. Quoted in Edward A. Steiner, *On the Trail of the Immigrant* (New York: Fleming H. Revell, 1900), 80.

27. "Name High Official in Immigrant Graft," *New York Times*, July 15, 1921; Unrau, *Historic Resource Study*, 2:277–278.

28. Quoted in Pitkin, *Keepers of the Gate*, 35–36.

29. Ibid., 36.

30. Quoted in ibid., 37.

31. Quoted in Unrau, *Historic Resource Study*, 2:224.

32. Quoted in Pitkin, *Keepers of the Gate*, 37.

33. Quoted in ibid., 95.

34. Unrau, *Historic Resource Study*, 2:257; Dr. Robert L. Leslie, interviewed by Dana Gumb, Aug. 14, 1985, Interview Number 017, Ellis Island Oral History Project, U.S. Department of the Interior, National Park Service; "Name High Official in Immigrant Graft," *New York Times*, July 15, 1921; Henry H. Curran, *Pillar to Post* (New York: Charles Scribner's Sons, 1941), 306–309.

35. Perkins quoted in Moreno, *Encyclopedia of Ellis Island*, 246–247.

36. Safford, *Immigration Problems*, 216–218.

37. Unrau, *Historic Resource Study*, 2:633.

38. Pitkin, *Keepers of the Gate*, 75–76.

39. "Missionary Accused of Deceiving Immigrants," *New York Times*, Oct. 11, 1902.

40. William Williams to the Austrian Society of New York, May 24, 1910, Box 7, Folder 93, Harlan D. Unrau Papers, Ellis Island Archives.

41. Quoted in Unrau, *Historic Resource Study*, 2:256.

42. "Ousts Aid Societies from Ellis Island," *New York Times*, Aug. 11, 1909; Moreno, *Encyclopedia of Ellis Island*, 48.

43. Pitkin, *Keepers of the Gate*, 75.

44. Watchorn quoted in ibid., 81–82.

45. Quoted in Unrau, *Historic Resource Study*, 2:221; Philip Cowen, *Memories of an American Jew* (New York: International Press, 1932), 151–152; Pitkin, *Keepers of the Gate*, 87–89, 39.

46. "Wallis Localizes Ellis Island Graft," *New York Times*, July 17, 1921.

47. Brandenburg, *Imported Americans*, 223–224.

48. Matrons of Ellis Island to William B. Wilson, secretary of labor, June 10, 1914, Box 7, Folder 109, Harlan D. Unrau Papers, Ellis Island Archives; Howe quoted in Unrau, *Historic Resource Study*, 3:737–738.

49. Unrau, *Historic Resource Study*, 3:738–739.

50. "Ellis Island Faces Strike," *New York Times*, Aug. 31, 1920; Unrau, *Historic Resource Study*, 2:291–292.

51. Quoted in Unrau, *Historic Resource Study*, 2:283–284.

52. Quoted in ibid., 2:557.

CHAPTER FIVE: How Immigrants Responded to Entering America and Changed the System

1. Louis Adamic, *Laughing in the Jungle: The Autobiography of an Immigrant in America* (New York: Harper and Brothers, 1932), 45.

2. Quoted in David M. Brownstone, Irene M. Franck, and Douglass L. Brownstone, *Island of Hope, Island of Tears* (New York: Rawson, Wade, 1979), 237, 257; Ida Levy quoted in Joan Morrison and Charlotte Fox Zabusky, *American Mosaic: The Immigrant Experience in the Words of Those Who Lived It* (Pittsburgh: University of

Pittsburgh Press, 1980), 103; William Reinhart, Abraham Livshein quoted in Peter Morton Coan, *Ellis Island Interviews* (New York: Barnes and Noble, 1997), 181, 161; Morris Shapiro quoted in Bruce M. Stave and John F. Sutherland with Aldo Salerno, *From the Old Country: An Oral History of European Migration to America* (New York: Twayne, 1994), 42.

3. Nils Sablin quoted in Stave and Sutherland with Salerno, *From the Old Country*, 48.

4. Quoted in Brownstone, Franck, and Brownstone, *Island of Hope*, 259–261.

5. Mrozowski quoted in Stave and Sutherland with Salerno, *From the Old Country*, 27; Edward Corsi, *In the Shadow of Liberty: The Chronicle of Ellis Island* (New York: MacMillan, 1935), 23–24.

6. Quoted in Brownstone, Franck, and Brownstone, *Island of Hope*, 240–241.

7. Quoted in ibid., 247.

8. Quoted in Erika Lee and Judy Yung, *Angel Island: Immigrant Gateway to America* (New York: Oxford University Press, 2010), 108.

9. Estelle Schwartz Belford, interviewed by Paul Sigrist, May 14, 1991, Excerpts of Interviews, Ellis Island Oral History Collection.

10. Quoted in Harlan D. Unrau, *The Historic Resource Study: Ellis Island–Statue of Liberty National Monument*, vol. 2 (Washington, DC: National Park Service, 1984), 290.

11. Quoted in Roger Daniels, *Coming to America: A History of Immigration and Ethnicity in American Life* (New York: Harper Perennial, 1990), 283.

12. Quoted in Unrau, *Historic Resource Study*, 3:917.

13. Henry H. Curran, *Pillar to Post* (New York: Charles Scribner's Sons, 1941), 287–288, 290–291.

14. Ibid., 297–298.

15. Quoted in ibid., 300.

16. Quoted in Lee and Yung, *Angel Island*, 49.

17. Curran, *Pillar to Post*, 298–299.

18. Quoted in ibid., 311.

19. Quoted in Thomas M. Pitkin, *Keepers of the Gate: A History of Ellis Island* (New York: New York University Press, 1975), 162; Corsi, *In the Shadow of Liberty*, 95, 97.

Epilogue

1. Quoted in Erika Lee and Judy Yung, *Angel Island: Immigrant Gateway to America* (New York: Oxford University Press, 2010), 304.

2. Quoted in ibid., 307.

3. Toy and Woolsey quoted in ibid., 310.

4. Quoted in Thomas M. Pitkin, *Keepers of the Gate: A History of Ellis Island* (New York: New York University Press, 1975), 173.

5. Ibid., 175.

6. Quoted in Vincent J. Cannato, *American Passage: The History of Ellis Island* (New York: HarperCollins, 2009), 381.

7. Quoted in ibid., 397.

8. Gary Gerstle, *American Crucible: Race and Nation in the Twentieth Century* (Princeton, NJ: Princeton University Press, 2001).

9. Quoted in *Atlanta Journal-Constitution*, Jan. 3, 2013.

10. Quoted in Peter Morton Coan, *Toward A Better Life: America's New Immigrants in Their Own Words—from Ellis Island to the Present* (Amherst, NY: Prometheus Books, 2011), 237.

11. Quoted in ibid., 265.

12. Quoted in Joan Morrison and Charlotte Fox Zabusky, *American Mosaic: The Immigrant Experience in the Words of Those Who Lived It* (Pittsburgh: University of Pittsburgh Press, 1980), 406.

SELECTED FURTHER READING

Ellis Island has been the subject of many publications, but for the purposes of this book, the most important sources have been the interviews with immigrants, doctors, aid workers, and others who lived the Ellis Island experience.

The Ellis Island archives have a good collection of oral histories of those who best knew the immigrant station, especially during the peak years. Also the Harlan D. Unrau Papers, which resulted in the three-volume *The Historic Resource Study: Ellis Island / Statue of Liberty National Monument* (1984) used in the preservation plans for Ellis Island, has valuable information on its legislative, statistical, administrative, and construction history, plus select reactions from individuals during the peak years. Unrau was a National Park Service historian. The Ellis Island Oral History Project, U.S. Department of the Interior, National Park Service has a large collection of oral histories available on microfilm. Also useful is the Ellis Island, National Park Service website, www.nps.gov/elis/index.htm, which provides historical facts, interviews, and other information for those studying Ellis Island.

Other primary sources include autobiographies and reminiscences penned by immigration commissioners, staff, doctors, and journalists. Among these are works by immigration commissioners such as John B. Weber's *Autobiography of John B. Weber* (1924), Robert Watchorn's *The Autobiography of Robert Watchorn* (1959), Frederic C. Howe's *The Confessions of a Reformer* (1925), Henry H. Curran's *Pillar to Post* (1941), and Edward Corsi's *In the Shadow of Liberty: The Chronicle of Ellis Island* (1935); descriptions from doctors such as Victor Safford's *Immigration Problems: Personal Experiences of an Official* (1925); Alfred C. Reed, "Going Through Ellis Island," *Popular Science Monthly* 82 (1913); Allan McLaughlin, "How Immigrants Are Inspected," *Popular Science Monthly* 66 (1905); inspector Philip Cowen's *Memories of an American Jew* (1932); and interpreter Fiorello H. La Guardia's *The Making of an Insurgent, an Autobiography: 1882–1919* ([1948] 1961). American journalists and others who traveled in steerage with the immigrants and went through processing offer excellent descriptions of the experience. Among these are Broughton Brandenburg, *Imported Americans: The Story of the Experience of a Disguised American and His Wife Studying the Immigration Question* (1904); and Edward A. Steiner, *On the Trail of The Immigrant* (1906).

Immigrants also left their impressions: see Louis Adamic, *Laughing in the Jungle: The Autobiography of an Immigrant in America* (1932); Marie Jastrow, *A Time to Remember: Growing Up in New York before the Great War* (1979); and Mary Antin, *The*

Promised Land (1912). Other works that provide oral histories, Ellis Island information, and other aspects of the immigrant experience which are very useful are Peter Morton Coan, *Ellis Island Interviews: Immigrants Tell Their Stories in Their Own Words* (1997), and his *Toward A Better Life: America's New Immigrants in Their Own Words—from Ellis Island to the Present* (2011); David M. Brownstone, Irene M. Franck, and Douglass L. Brownstone, *Island of Hope, Island of Tears* (1979); Emmy E. Werner, *Passages to America: Oral Histories of Child Immigrants from Ellis Island and Angel Island* (2009); Michael La Sorte, *La Merica: Images of Italian Greenhorn Experience* (1985); Joan Morrison and Charlotte Fox Zabusky, *American Mosaic: The Immigrant Experience in the Words of Those Who Lived It* (1980); Irving Howe, *World of Our Fathers* (1976); Sydney Stahl Weinberg, *The World of Our Mothers: The Lives of Jewish Immigrant Women* (1988); and Bertha May Boody, *A Psychological Study of Immigrant Children at Ellis Island* (1926).

Ellis Island's history is covered best and in great detail in Vincent J. Cannato, *American Passage: The History of Ellis Island* (2009); and Thomas M. Pitkin, *Keepers of the Gate: A History of Ellis Island* (1975). In a separate category is Barry Moreno's *Encyclopedia of Ellis Island* (2004), which provides all the information a reader might want to know about the station in alphabetically ordered entries.

Specialized studies that are invaluable include Alan M. Kraut, *Silent Travelers: Germs, Genes, and the "Immigrant Menace"* (1994); Amy L. Fairchild, *Science at the Borders: Immigrant Medical Inspection and the Shaping of the Modern Industrial Labor Force* (2003); and Lorie Conway, *Forgotten Ellis Island: The Extraordinary Story of America's Immigrant Hospital* (2007).

The best books on Angel Island are Erika Lee and Judy Yung, *Angel Island: Immigrant Gateway to America* (2010); Erika Lee, *At America's Gates: Chinese Immigration during the Exclusion Era, 1882–1943* (2003); Robert Eric Barde, *Immigration at the Golden Gate: Passenger Ships, Exclusion, and Angel Island* (2008); and for the poetry written on Angel Island walls, Him Mark Lai, Genny Lin, and Judy Yung, *Island: Poetry and History of Chinese Immigrants on Angel Island, 1910–1940* (1980).

For general immigration history of the late nineteenth and early twentieth century, the best coverage is in Roger Daniels, *Coming to America: A History of Immigration and Ethnicity in American Life* (1990), and his *Guarding the Golden Door: American Immigration Policy and Immigrants since 1882* (2004); as well as Alan Kraut, *The Huddled Masses: The Immigrant in American Society, 1880–1921* (1982).

INDEX

Page numbers in *italics* refer to photographs.